BE YOUR OWN
Astrologer

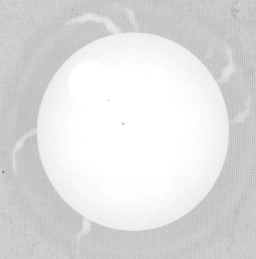

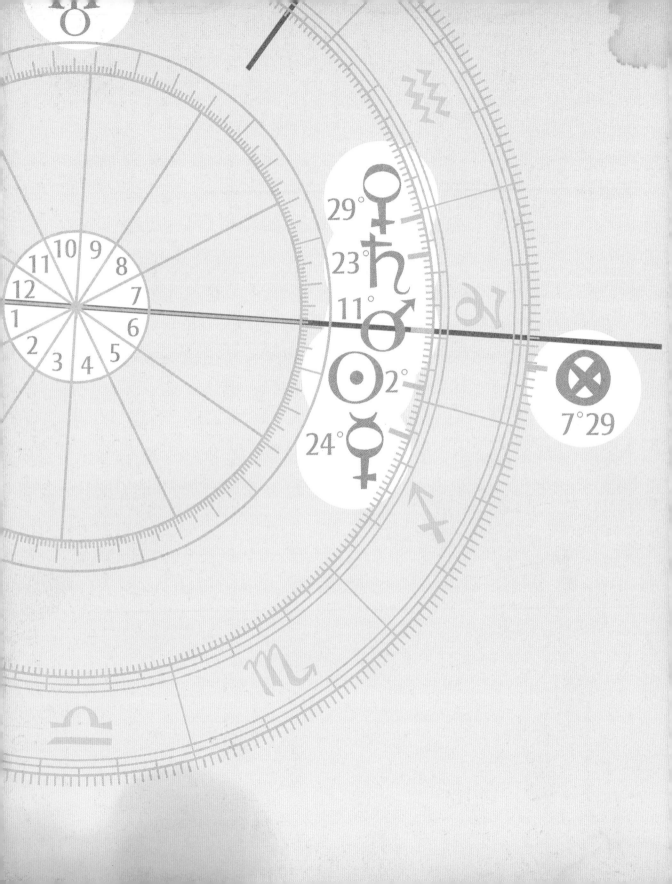

BE YOUR OWN
Astrologer

STEP BY STEP TO CREATING AND
INTERPRETING YOUR BIRTH CHART

Paul Wade

STERLING

New York / London
www.sterlingpublishing.com

To all of my students, clients and friends.
To mad Aquarians and to bleating Capricorns.

Library of Congress Cataloging-in-Publication Data Available

10 9 8 7 6 5 4 3 2

Published in 2006 by Sterling Publishing Co., Inc.
387 Park Avenue South, New York, NY 10016

First published in the UK by Godsfield Press
A division of Octopus Publishing Group Ltd
© 2006 by Octopus Publishing Group Ltd

Distributed in Canada by Sterling Publishing
c/o Canadian Manda Group, 165 Dufferin Street
Toronto, Ontario, Canada M6K 3H6

Printed in China

Sterling ISBN-13: 978-1-4027-3601-8
        ISBN-10: 1-4027-3601-0

For information about custom editions, special sales,
premium and corporate purchases, please contact
Sterling Special Sales Department at 800-805-5489 or
specialsales@sterlingpub.com.

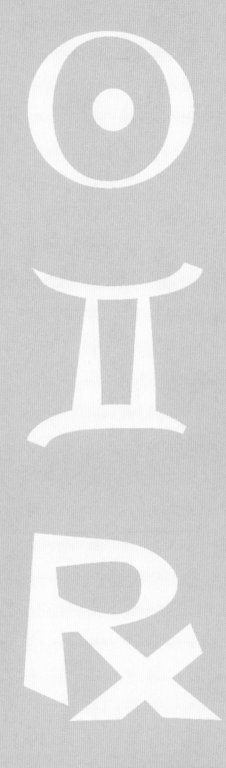

CONTENTS

INTRODUCTION

ASTROLOGY AND YOU

This book is for those who are fascinated by the mysteries of astrology and eager to learn more. The pages that follow will guide you through the calculation and construction of your own astrological birth chart and the step-by-step analysis and interpretation of what you'll find.

If you have ever been impressed by the accuracy of astrologers in the media, that is nothing compared to the insights awaiting you once you are able to interpret your own chart. It is a skill that, once learned, you'll always remember, and working on what is effectively your own cosmic self-portrait is often a deeply therapeutic, enlightening and enjoyable experience.

An astrological birth chart is a symbolic representation of the heavens for the time and the place of your birth. It is almost certainly completely unique to you, since even between twins there will always be subtle differences. As you work out and then analyze your own birth chart, you can't help but gain a great understanding of planetary dynamics and of the ponderous machinations of our universe. You'll connect directly with a long line of celestial observers and with a body of knowledge that has been built and passed

down through the ages, and it is certain that your own world view will be altered forever.

Opposite is a blank birth chart template. You will need to use this blank chart whenever you draw your own or somebody else's chart. It is a good idea to photocopy the blank chart onto some interestingly colored or textured paper for the most intriguing impact. The circular section at the top of the chart will contain a symbolic view of the sky at the time of your birth and the tables at the bottom will present a breakdown of this information.

Over the chapters that follow, you will learn to determine how the heavens appeared at the instant of your birth and what this means for your personal happiness, career, relationships, wealth, life and sense of self-fulfillment. Subsequently, your knowledge can be applied to understanding those around you—a great advantage!

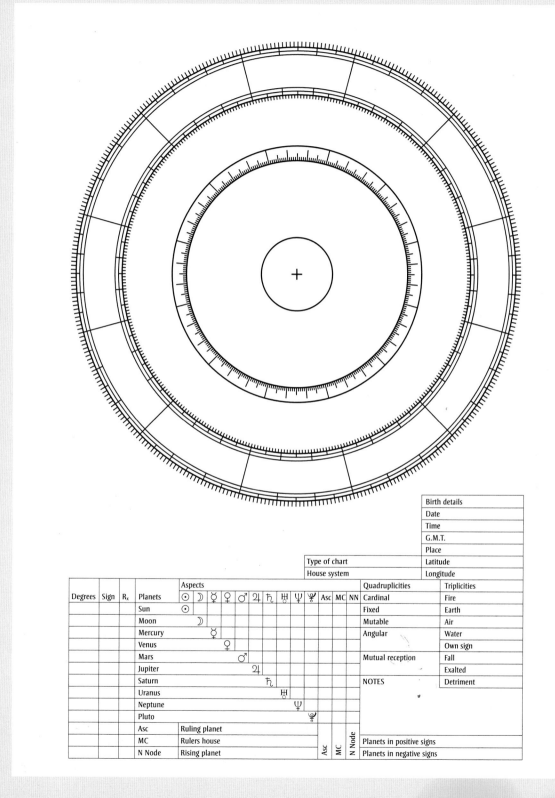

Birth details	
Date	
Time	
G.M.T.	
Place	
Type of chart	Latitude
House system	Longitude

Degrees	Sign	Rₓ	Planets	Aspects ☉ ☽ ☿ ♀ ♂ ♃ ♄ ♅ ♆ ♇ Asc MC NN	Quadruplicities	Triplicities
			Sun ☉		Cardinal	Fire
			Moon ☽		Fixed	Earth
			Mercury ☿		Mutable	Air
			Venus ♀		Angular	Water
			Mars ♂			Own sign
			Jupiter ♃		Mutual reception	Fall
			Saturn ♄			Exalted
			Uranus ♅		NOTES	Detriment
			Neptune ♆			
			Pluto ♇			
			Asc	Ruling planet		
			MC	Rulers house	Planets in positive signs	
			N Node	Rising planet	Planets in negative signs	

Asc   MC   N Node

HOW TO USE THIS BOOK

This book is a complete guide to calculating and interpreting your own unique astrological birth chart. Worksheets and sources of reference are provided at every stage of the calculation process to make things easy for you and the structured and methodical approach to drawing and interpreting your chart will help you get the most from your analysis. If you work through the book systematically you will gain a solid foundation of astrological knowledge. Alternatively, if you don't feel like practicing your calculations, you will still learn a lot from reading Understanding your Birth Chart (see pages 56–139).

CREATING YOUR BIRTH CHART

The first part of the book shows you how you can work out the position of your planets, houses and rising sign from just your time, date and place of birth.

- **Calculate Your Chart** (see pages 20–39) provides step-by-step instructions to help you calculate your birth chart. Each stage of the process is accompanied by easy-to-use worksheets and worked examples to help you understand what you are doing.

- **Draw Your Birth Chart** (see pages 40–55) shows you how to take the information you calculated in Chapter 1 and draw it onto your chart.

UNDERSTANDING YOUR BIRTH CHART

The second part of the book has been specially designed to help you build your understanding of astrology.

- **Interpretation Essentials** (see pages 58–93) explores the meaning of the houses, signs, planets and angles and explains what they mean individually and together.

- **First Impressions** (see pages 94–105) provides a holistic view of your birth chart and considers the meaning of the chart shape, distribution of planets and aspect patterns.

- **Interpreting Your Planets** (see pages 106–113) will help you to understand and analyze your planetary positions and interpret your rising and ruling planets, unaspected planets and other planetary placings.

- **Special Features** (see pages 114–127) helps you to delve deeper into your interpretation. It covers the moon's nodes, the Part of Fortune, Chiron, the chart signature and planets in anaretic positions and void of course.

- **Working with Astrology** (see pages 128–139) presents further techniques for understanding your chart. You'll learn how to make predictions with transits and progressions and how to understand your relationships using synastry and the composite chart.

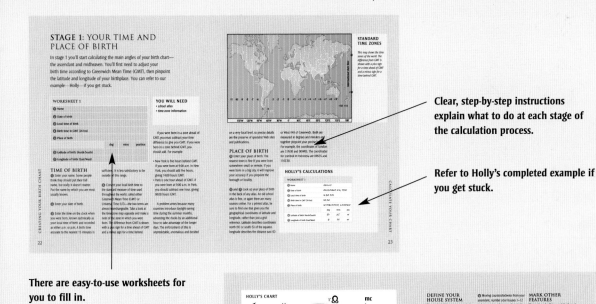

STAGE 1: YOUR TIME AND PLACE OF BIRTH

Clear, step-by-step instructions explain what to do at each stage of the calculation process.

Refer to Holly's completed example if you get stuck.

There are easy-to-use worksheets for you to fill in.

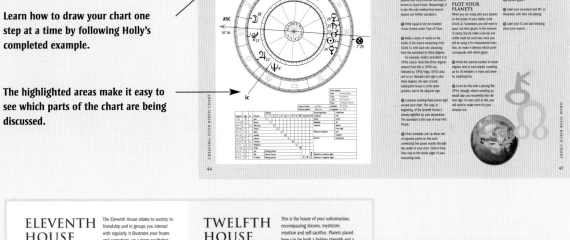

HOLLY'S CHART

Learn how to draw your chart one step at a time by following Holly's completed example.

The highlighted areas make it easy to see which parts of the chart are being discussed.

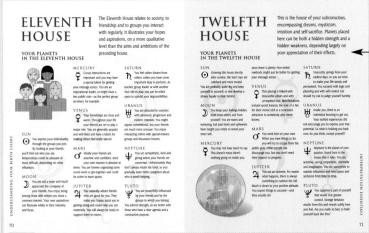

ELEVENTH HOUSE

The Eleventh House relates to society, to friendship and to groups you interact with regularly. It illustrates your hopes and aspirations, on a more qualitative level than the aims and ambitions of the preceding house.

TWELFTH HOUSE

This is the house of your subconscious, encompassing dreams, mysticism, intuition and self-sacrifice. Planets placed here can be both a hidden strength and a hidden weakness, depending largely on your appreciation of their effects.

Discover what your chart means by reading the detailed interpretations for each planet, house, sign, aspect and angle.

BACKGROUND TO ASTROLOGY

For most people, "astrology" means reading their stars in the paper, those few lines based around your month of birth. If you are typical, you will tend to remember your forecast when it is good and dismiss it when it seems less encouraging—although almost everyone can think of at least one occasion when a brief comment from a media astrologer, addressed to millions of people all over the world, has seemed so directly relevant to their own personal situation that they might even have made a life-altering decision as a result.

YOUR BIRTH CHART

So how can predictions be made solely on the month of your birth, and is there any way to improve their accuracy consistently? The answer is that by concentrating more finely on the circumstances surrounding your birth, highlighting a unique set of criteria that are much more specific, a far more individual cosmic picture can be drawn that could prove even more startling.

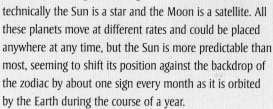

In total there are nine planets in our solar system. For astrological purposes we are observing this from the Earth, so eight planets remain in view. The Sun and the Moon are also included as planets by astrologers, although technically the Sun is a star and the Moon is a satellite. All these planets move at different rates and could be placed anywhere at any time, but the Sun is more predictable than most, seeming to shift its position against the backdrop of the zodiac by about one sign every month as it is orbited by the Earth during the course of a year.

This means that the position of the Sun is quite easy to anticipate, since it moves quickly enough to have a definable impact and slowly enough not to be unnoticed. However, ultimately it is only one planet out of ten, so for a media forecast to be even as much as one tenth accurate is really a remarkable achievement.

Think how much better it would be if you had cast every planetary position for yourself, along with an assessment of your astrological houses, your rising sign, and a whole multitude of other chart features (more on what these are later!). Once you have done this you can really get astrology working for you.

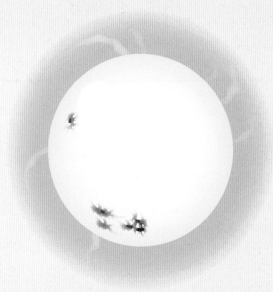

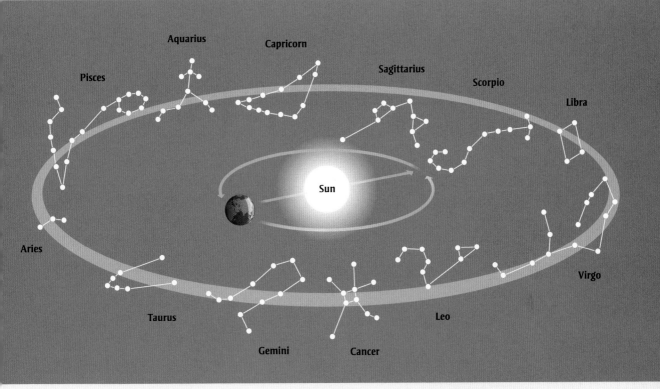

ORIGINS

The origins of astrology have been lost over time, but
certainly stretch back several millennia to a period pre-dating
much recorded history. If you have ever wondered about
how such distant celestial bodies can have an impact on our
everyday lives, try thinking for a moment about the Moon.
The Moon consistently moves the tides of the vast oceans,
yet we are supposedly immune from its effects, although
water is by far the biggest single constituent of our brains
and bodies. Or consider the Sun, which drives the seasons
and without which there would be no life on Earth at all.

   Thus, rather than asking how the planets might affect our
lives, it is often more reasonable to begin by considering
how they could possibly not. The lives of many plants and
animals are tied in inextricably with planetary cycles so it is
surely arrogant to presume that we ourselves are immune to
their effects.

HOW ASTROLOGY CAN HELP YOU

Astrology is useful for figuring out what sort of day you're going to have, for anticipating helpful trends and for letting you spot pitfalls in good time. But what about drawing your own birth chart, sometimes called your horoscope (a word that derives from two Greek words meaning "to observe the time")? What else can you learn from what is, after all, a complicated undertaking?

First, you will learn plenty about geography, the measurement of time, planetary orbits and celestial mechanics during the calculation phase. Second, you will learn a lot about astrological symbolism, a symbolic language for better understanding ourselves. Third, once you interpret your birth chart, the deeper you go the more amazed you will be by what you find.

The different facets of an astrological interpretation reflect the complex nature of human existence and the many different *sub-personalities* that combine to create who we are. You'll probably find your birth chart seems full of contradictions, with how you think, feel and behave in one situation often radically different from your responses in the next.

Drawing and studying your own chart will help you to take an objective overview of all these disparate influences, to identify and emphasize the things that make you happiest, and to deal constructively with those that would perhaps benefit from moderation, a review of their purpose, or channelling into a more constructive direction.

FINDING A DIRECTION

For many people life is a serious and hectic business, with little time for contemplation or to stand back and question what it's all about. Astrology can help with pinpointing the most appropriate direction for you. Are you a career person who needs a home, for example, or are you a home-oriented person who would like a career? Should you devote yourself to family matters, to the world of work, or is there a more independent path for you? Which jobs might be best and under what circumstances would you work most effectively? What about traveling? Or education? Or your health? An astrological investigation of your birth chart can help highlight the best approach, in all these matters and more.

One area where astrology is especially helpful is in our relationships. Those who are immediately able to establish harmonious and long-lasting partnerships are nowadays in the minority, with many people repeating the same mistakes, falling for the wrong people, getting involved in impossible triangles, becoming overcommitted too quickly, or feeling trapped when involved and lonely on their own, to name but a few.

Examining your birth chart can help you to separate those characteristics to which you are simply attracted from those that you actually need in a potential partner. It can help you to understand the ways in which problematic patterns of relating might be established early in life—with your parents, for example, the first people you encountered this closely. The benefits of reassessing these issues are often immeasurable, reflecting especially in improved adult relationships as a result.

ASTROLOGICAL SYMBOLISM

To save having to write out the name of a planet or constellation over and over again, astrologers have developed a kind of shorthand, using glyphs or symbols. These are covered in the following charts, and it's useful to familiarize yourself with them before you begin calculating and interpreting your birth chart.

SIGNS

Every sign has a glyph (or symbol) that you can use to show where it is positioned.

ARIES

 Symbolized by the Ram, you can think of the Aries glyph as the Ram's horns.

TAURUS

 Symbolized by the Bull, you can see the Bull's head clearly in the Taurus glyph.

GEMINI

The Roman numeral for two is the glyph for Gemini, the Heavenly Twins.

CANCER

 The Crab's eyes peer cautiously from his shell, helping to remind us of Cancer.

LEO

 The glyph for Leo could be the Lion's mane, but perhaps it is more like his tail.

VIRGO

 Virgo's symbol says "M" for Maiden. Don't ever mix it up with Scorpio's glyph.

LIBRA

 In mathematics, this same Libran symbol means "approximately equal to."

SCORPIO

 Think of the sting in the Scorpion's tail and you'll always remember this glyph.

SAGITTARIUS

 Sagittarius is the centaur Archer and a stout arrow represents this sign.

CAPRICORN

 Capricorn the Sea-Goat has a curly fish's tail, merging with a goat's head.

AQUARIUS

 Optimistic Water-Bearers will start and end their glyph on an upward stroke.

PISCES

These two Fish are kissing. It is better than swimming in opposite directions!

PLANETS

Each planet also has a unique glyph. These are used by astrologers to pinpoint the position of the planets in your chart. Planets are marked according to their placing within each sign and in the zodiac as a whole. It will save you a lot of time if you can remember these glyphs!

SUN

 This glyph reminds us of the central position the Sun enjoys in our solar system. Everybody orbits this hub.

MOON

 The symbol for the Moon is unmistakable. Some prefer this to face left while others prefer it to face right.

MERCURY

 Mercury, or Hermes, was the messenger of the gods. He wore a distinctive winged hat, highlighted in this glyph.

VENUS

 The astrological glyph for Venus is used widely to represent the female gender as a whole.

MARS

 The glyph for Mars is often used to signify the male gender. As god of war, might this hint at something?

JUPITER

 The glyph for Jupiter combines the figures two and four. An extravagant flourish completes this figure.

SATURN

 Looking like a curly letter "h," the symbol for Saturn is similar to that of Jupiter, but is rotated and inverted.

URANUS

 Uranus rules television and new technology, so visualize this glyph as a planet with a TV aerial on top!

NEPTUNE

 Neptune was the mythological god of the sea, distinguished by his trident, a three-pointed fish spear.

PLUTO

 Pluto's symbol looks a little like that for Neptune. You may sometimes see it shown as the letters P and L combined, to remind us of Pluto and of Percival Lowell, whose work laid the foundation for the discovery of this planet.

MAJOR ASPECTS

The zodiac is a circle that is made up of 360 degrees. Because there are 12 signs in the zodiac, each one comprises 30 degrees. When planets are placed a certain distance apart in the zodiac, a dynamic influence takes effect that changes the impact of any planets thus connected. Aspects are angular relationships between planets, or between other features in your chart.

Some aspects are helpful and are called *soft*, while others prove more difficult and are termed *hard*. All can be managed so as to highlight their positive side. Details for measuring and recording your aspects are found later in this chapter, and some ideas for aspect interpretation are given in Chapter 3 (see pages 58–93).

CONJUNCTION
(0 degrees, hard aspect)

 Remember the glyph for a conjunction as half a dumbbell, or maybe one half of the opposition symbol. Planets in exact conjunction are right next to one another. A conjunction is best seen as a hard aspect.

SEXTILE
(60 degrees, soft aspect)

 The sextile glyph resembles a snowflake, with six or maybe eight points. Two features in sextile are 60 degrees, the space of two signs apart. This is a soft and helpful aspect, which takes a little effort to work at its best.

SQUARE
(90 degrees, hard aspect)

The symbol for a square is, well, a square! The square is a challenging aspect. Two planets in square are at right angles to one another, that is three signs and 90 degrees apart.

TRINE
(120 degrees, soft aspect)

A triangle represents a trine. Sometimes three trines will link up around your chart to form a large triangular pattern. The trine is a soft aspect, showing two features 120 degrees, four signs or one third of the birth chart apart.

OPPOSITION
(180 degrees, hard aspect)

The glyph for an opposition looks like a dumbbell. Imagine two planets on opposite sides of the horoscope. The opposition is a hard aspect, having consequences perceived often as external.

MINOR ASPECTS

As well as the five major aspects, there are many others, usually considered to be of reduced significance. The inconjunct is definitely the most popular of these and is most often noted. A maximum of two degrees either side of exactitude is permissible for any minor aspect as its *orb of influence*—the maximum extent to which an impact can be felt. Beyond this, any effect is disregarded.

INCONJUNCT
(150 degrees, hard aspect)

Sometimes known as the quincunx, the inconjunct shows two planets five signs apart, or with 150 degrees between them. Often stressful at first, over time this aspect can encourage self-awareness and development.

SEMI-SEXTILE
(30 degrees, soft aspect)

Weighing in at 30 degrees of separation, the semi-sextile shows planets that are one sign apart from each other. Its effects are moderately useful and, as you might have guessed, about half as helpful as a sextile.

SEMI-SQUARE
(45 degrees, hard aspect)

The semi-square not only looks a bit like half a square, it has a span of just 45 degrees and an impact that is about half as powerful.

SESQUIQUADRATE
(135 degrees, hard aspect)

The sesquiquadrate is like a square and a half both in terms of its glyph and its angular separation. Its impact, though, is weaker, more like that of a semi-square than any more powerful in consequence.

QUINTILE
(72 degrees, hard aspect)

Quintiles divide the birth chart by five, resulting in a distance of 72 degrees. They are stressful, but are linked with creativity and with the desire to change things.

BIQUINTILE
(144 degrees, hard aspect)

Two planets separated by 144 degrees are in biquintile aspect. The effect is again a creative one, although often seen as rather weak.

OTHER SYMBOLISM

Here are some other important symbols that you will need to know.

ASCENDANT

asc The ascendant is the constellation rising over the eastern horizon at the moment of your birth. It is sometimes called your rising sign.

MIDHEAVEN

mc The midheaven is the point of upper culmination, the highest point reached by the planets, between rising and setting. The initials stand for medium coeli, from the Latin meaning "middle of the sky."

IMUM COELI

ic The imum coeli, or IC, is the point of lower culmination and is opposite from the midheaven. The name in Latin means "the bottom part of the sky."

CHIRON

Chiron is a quasi-dormant comet, captured between Saturn and Uranus in the icy fringes of the outer solar system. Only found in 1977, Chiron has become very important over the past few years.

RETROGRADE

Astrology looks at the solar system from the Earth. In reality, though, everything is orbiting the Sun, so planets can overtake us if they move fast enough, or we can do the same to them. From our perspective this leads to retrograde motion, when the planet seems to move backward as a result.

MOON'S NORTH NODE

The main point of intersection of the Earth's orbit around the Sun and the Moon's orbit around the Earth. There is more nodal astronomy in Chapter 1—and much more nodal interpretation in Chapter 6!

PART OF FORTUNE

Based around your own unique Sun, Moon and ascendant positions, the Part of Fortune shows where and how you will find joy and happiness. Calculation and interpretation details are as with the nodes.

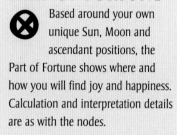

CREATING YOUR BIRTH CHART

♎ ♏ ♐ ♑ ♒ ♓

There are two main stages to creating your own birth chart. First, you need to work out the positions of the planets and zodiac constellations when you were born, remembering that these celestial features move over time and also differ in position according to where you were born. Then, you need to record this information on your horoscope wheel— a symbolic representation of the sky for the time and location of your birth.

♎ ♏ ♐ ♑ ♒ ♓

CALCULATE YOUR CHART

GETTING STARTED

For some the thought of calculating anything is distressing. Perhaps this was not your best subject at school and you have lasting bad memories. Yet you probably use mathematics every day in your normal life, as you work out how much gas to put in your car, how much your income changes year to year or how much you can afford to spend on a night out.

YOU WILL NEED
- midnight ephemeris (see page 21)
- table of houses (see page 21)
- atlas (see page 23)
- scientific calculator (see below)
- pen
- colored pens
- pencil
- ruler
- eraser
- compasses
- correcting fluid

No stage of birth chart calculation is really any more difficult than any of these tasks. There are lots of stages, but by working methodically you will arrive at your finished calculations without hurting too badly. This chapter contains detailed worksheets to guide you through the calculation process.

You can either complete them here, or copy them first for your family and friends. You will then become a member of that select group able to calculate a birth chart for themselves!

SCIENTIFIC CALCULATOR
Our main concession to modern technology is the scientific calculator. Previously, astrologers used logarithms, but powerful calculators are now cheap and widely available. For a minimal outlay you can get a scientific calculator with a degrees key, labeled [DMS] or something similar, which

will enable you to work directly with degrees, minutes and seconds as a measure of space or hours, minutes and seconds as a measurement of time. These calculators are recommended for school students and so are easy to get hold of from stationers and similar stores. Full instructions on working with your degrees key will accompany your calculator and may differ slightly depending on the model.

With a little trial and error using the example calculations, you will soon be on your way. Remember always to think in columns as you enter your data, so if, for example, you want to enter four minutes you should be telling your calculator:

0 [DMS] 4 [DMS] 0 [DMS]

And to enter ten seconds, you should type in the following:

0 [DMS] 0 [DMS] 10 [DMS]

Mixing up these columns is by far the biggest cause of calculation inaccuracies. Just entering ten or four makes your calculator believe you are talking either in hours or in whole degrees.

MIDNIGHT EPHEMERIS

An ephemeris is a book listing planetary positions for a given period, usually for one year or for one century. Those covering a whole century are the most economical to buy, although now that we're on the cusp of the millennium you'll need to get two editions, one for the 20th century and a second for the 21st. Ephemerides are also published in both midnight and noon formats, depending on the time of day for which positions are listed. The former are easier to use, so all the calculations here are based around the use of a midnight edition.

EXTRACT FROM TABLE OF HOUSES

Sidereal time			10 ♓	Ascendant ♋
Hours	Mins	Secs	Degrees°	Degrees°
22	34	54	7°	10°16
22	38	40	8°	11°02

The American Ephemeris is probably the most widely used. It is published by Astro Computing Services (ACS) in San Diego, California, in two volumes, one for the 20th century and a second for 21st, actually covering the period until 2050. Be sure when making your purchase to specify the midnight edition of both ephemerides.

TABLES OF HOUSES

Tables of houses are published for different latitudes and locations. They give the placing of the ascendant and midheaven at different sidereal times. Usually these tables are intended for use with a particular method of house division, with each house relating to a specific part of your life. You'll be using the Equal House method, one of the oldest, most versatile and most straightforward systems to grasp.

Any table of houses works for Equal House, even one aligned with Placidus or Koch, to name a couple of popular rivals. Some tables of houses are labeled as for the northern hemisphere, when, with a simple conversion (see pages 25 and 27), they will function equally well in the southern hemisphere. A good table of houses is published by the Rosicrucian Fellowship. It gives houses for one-degree increments on the midheaven.

EXTRACT FROM EPHEMERIS

Day	Sidereal time			Sun			Moon			Mercury			Venus			Mars			Jupiter			Saturn			Uranus			Neptune			Pluto			North Node		
	Hours	Mins	Secs	Deg	Min	Sign (%)	Deg	Min	Sign (%)	Deg	Min	Sign (%)	Deg	Min	Sign (%)	Deg	Min	Sign (%)	Deg	Min	Sign (%)	Deg	Min	Sign (%)	Deg	Min	Sign (%)	Deg	Min	Sign (%)	Deg	Min	Sign (%)	Deg	Min	Sign (%)
24	6	6	14	1	13	♉	19	31	♊	25	4	♐	27	44	♉	10	35	♉	22	18	♌℞	22	50	♉	15	26	♑℞	7	56	♍℞	21	29	♋℞	0	42	♈
25	6	10	11	2	14	♉	2	32	♋	23	53	♐	28	59	♉	11	21	♉	22	15	♌℞	22	57	♉	15	26	♑℞	7	56	♍℞	21	28	♋℞	0	39	♈

STAGE 1: YOUR TIME AND PLACE OF BIRTH

In stage 1 you'll start calculating the main angles of your birth chart—the ascendant and midheaven. You'll first need to adjust your birth time according to Greenwich Mean Time (GMT), then pinpoint the latitude and longitude of your birthplace. You can refer to our example—Holly—if you get stuck.

WORKSHEET 1

	deg	mins	position
1 Name			
2 Date of birth			
3 Local time of birth			
4 Birth time in GMT (24 hrs)			
5 Place of birth			
6 Latitude of birth (North/South)			
7 Longitude of birth (East/West)			

YOU WILL NEED
- school atlas
- time-zone information

If you were born in a zone ahead of GMT, you must subtract your time difference to give you GMT. If you were born in a zone behind GMT, you should add. For example:

- New York is five hours behind GMT. If you were born at 9:00 a.m. in New York, you should add five hours, giving 14:00 hours GMT.
- Paris is one hour ahead of GMT. If you were born at 9:00 a.m. in Paris, you should subtract one hour, giving 08:00 hours GMT.

A problem arises because many countries introduce daylight-saving time during the summer months, advancing the clocks by an additional hour to take advantage of the longer days. The enforcement of this is unpredictable, anomalous and decided

TIME OF BIRTH

1 Enter your name. Some people think they should put their full name, but really it doesn't matter. Put the name by which you are most usually known.

2 Enter your date of birth.

3 Enter the time on the clock when you were born, known technically as your local time of birth and recorded as either a.m. or p.m. A birth time accurate to the nearest 15 minutes is

sufficient. It is less satisfactory to be outside of this range.

4 Convert your local birth time to the standard measure of time used throughout the world, called either Greenwich Mean Time (GMT) or Universal Time (UT)—the two terms are almost interchangeable. Take a look at the time zone map opposite and make a note of the zone in which you were born. The difference from GMT is shown with a plus sign for a time ahead of GMT and a minus sign for a time behind.

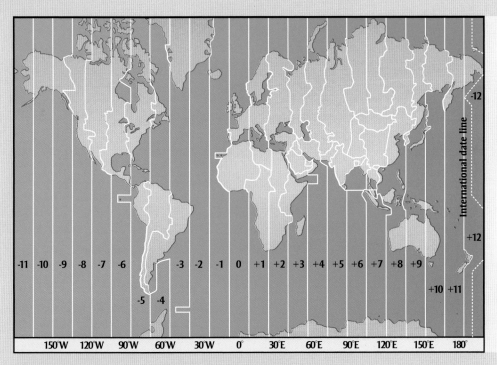

STANDARD TIME ZONES

This map shows the time zones of the world. The difference from GMT is shown with a plus sign for a time ahead of GMT and a minus sign for a time behind GMT.

on a very local level, so precise details are the preserve of specialist Web sites and publications.

PLACE OF BIRTH

5 Enter your place of birth. The nearest town is fine if you were born somewhere small or remote. If you were born in a big city, it will improve your accuracy if you pinpoint the borough or locality.

6 and **7** Look up your place of birth in the back of any atlas. An old school atlas is fine, or again there are many sources online. For a printed atlas, be sure to find one that gives you the geographical coordinates of latitude and longitude, rather than just a grid reference. Latitude describes coordinates north (N) or south (S) of the equator, longitude describes the distance east (E)

or West (W) of Greenwich. Both are measured in degrees and minutes and together pinpoint your precise location. For example, the coordinates of London are 51N30 and 00W05. The coordinates for Lombok in Indonesia are 08S35 and 116E30.

HOLLY'S CALCULATIONS

WORKSHEET 1			
1 Name	HOLLY		
2 Date of birth	DECEMBER 24, 1931		
3 Local time of birth	4:30 P.M.		
4 Birth time in GMT (24 hrs)	16:30		
5 Place of birth	WIMBLEDON, LONDON		
	deg	mins	pos
6 Latitude of birth (North/South)	51	25	N
7 Longitude of birth (East/West)	0	12	W

STAGE 2: CELESTIAL BIRTH TIME

In stage 2, you'll calculate the celestial or *sidereal* time for the time and the place of your birth. Sidereal ("sigh-deer-ial") time reflects the actual time it takes for the Earth to revolve on its axis. A sidereal day lasts 23 hours, 56 minutes and 4.09 seconds.

SIDEREAL TIME

1 Find your date of birth in the ephemeris and look for the column that gives the sidereal time. This refers to midnight on your birthday and at the Greenwich meridian, or zero degrees of longitude. Write the time in hours, minutes and seconds on your worksheet.

2 Copy your birth time expressed as GMT from worksheet 1 on page 22.

3 To work out your sidereal time of birth, you need to make a few adjustments. First, add your GMT birth time to the sidereal time at midnight on your birthday. Write your total here.

4 Since a sidereal day is shorter than a 24-hour day, each sidereal hour passes slightly more quickly. Because the whole day passes four minutes more quickly, each hour passes ten seconds faster. Using your scientific calculator, multiply your GMT birth time by ten seconds to reflect this and write the answer on your worksheet. Astrologers call this figure the *Acceleration on the Interval*.

WORKSHEET 2

	hours	mins	secs
1 Sidereal time at midnight			
2 GMT birth time			
3 Add answer for step 1 to answer for step 2			
4 Multiply GMT birth time by 10 secs			
5 Add answer for step 3 to answer for step 4			
6 Multiply birth longitude by 4 minutes			
7 Add/subtract answer for step 5 to/from answer for step 6			
8 Add 12 hours if born in Southern Latitude			
9 If LST more than 24 hours, subtract 24 hours 00 mins 00 secs			
10 Local sidereal birth time (LSBT)			

⑤ Now add columns 3 and 4. Your running total is the sidereal time for your moment of birth, but not yet for the location.

PLACE

⑥ Time is measured clockwise around the world, so it is later by the stars if you travel east and earlier if you travel west, as any air traveler experiences. The Earth is also a traveler in space. It rotates 360º in 24 hours, or one cycle of day and night. In celestial terms, this rotation equates to a turn of one degree every four sidereal minutes.

To account for the rotation of the Earth in sidereal terms, multiply your birth longitude by four minutes using your scientific calculator and write the result on your worksheet. Your answer is called the *Longitude Equivalent in Time*.

⑦ Now look at your answer for step 7 in Worksheet 1. If you were born in an easterly longitude relative to the Greenwich Meridian, you have an "E" after your answer. If so, add the figure in step 6 of this worksheet to step 5. If you were born in a westerly longitude, as Holly was, subtract the figure in step 6 of this worksheet from step 5. Note your running total. You have almost completed this stage . . .

⑧ If you were born in the Northern Hemisphere, you can ignore this step, but if you were born in the Southern Hemisphere, you'll need to make an adjustment here. If there is an "S" after your birth latitude in step 6 of worksheet 1, add a correction factor of 12 hours to your total now.

⑨ If your running total is greater than 24 hours, subtract 24 from your total, since you have effectively run into the next sidereal day. If your total is not over 24 hours, as is the case for Holly, you can skip this step. For the purposes of calculating your birth chart, it doesn't matter in which sidereal day you are. It is the actual time that counts.

⑩ Your answer is the local sidereal time for your time and place of birth. As you will see in the next step, it is the basis for orientating your horoscope.

HOLLY'S CALCULATIONS

WORKSHEET 2

	hours	mins	secs
① Sidereal time at midnight	6	6	14
② GMT birth time	16	30	–
③ Add answer for step 1 to answer for step 2	22	36	14
④ Multiply GMT birth time by 10 secs	–	2	45
⑤ Add answer for step 3 to answer for step 4	22	38	59
⑥ Multiply birth longitude by 4 minutes	0	0	48
⑦ Add/subtract answer for step 5 to/from answer for step 6	22	38	11
⑧ Add 12 hours if born in Southern Latitude	–	–	–
⑨ If LST more than 24 hours, subtract 24 hours 00 mins 00 secs	–	–	–
⑩ Local sidereal birth time (LSBT)	22	38	11

EXTRACT FROM EPHEMERIS

Day	Sidereal time			Sun			Moon			Mercury			Venus			Mars			Jupiter			Saturn			Uranus			Neptune			Pluto			North Node		
	Hours	Mins	Secs	Deg	Min	Sign	Deg	Min	Sign	Deg	Min	Sign	Deg	Min	Sign	Deg	Min	Sign	Deg	Min	Sign	Deg	Min	Sign	Deg	Min	Sign	Deg	Min	Sign	Deg	Min	Sign	Deg	Min	Sign
24	6	6	14	1	13	♉	19	31	♊	25	4	♐	27	44	♉	10	35	♉	22	18	♎R	22	50	♉	15	26	♑R	7	56	♍R	21	29	♋R	0	42	♈
25	6	10	11	2	14	♉	2	32	♋	23	53	♐	28	59	♉	11	21	♉	22	15	♎R	22	57	♉	15	26	♑R	7	56	♍R	21	28	♋R	0	39	♈

STAGE 3: FIND YOUR ASCENDANT AND MIDHEAVEN

Stage 3 is where you determine the whole orientation of your chart. It involves working out your ascendant and midheaven from your sidereal time of birth.

YOU WILL NEED
- scientific calculator
- tables of houses

FROM TABLE OF HOUSES

1 Choose the nearest latitude to your birthplace and enter it at the top of Step 3. A table of houses for London is used for Holly (see opposite).

2 From the table of houses for this nearest latitude, find and enter the *nearest later* sidereal time to your local sidereal time at birth (the figure you entered in step 10 of the worksheet 2 on page 24).

WORKSHEET 3

	hours	mins	secs	
1 Nearest latitude to birthplace			degrees	minutes
2 Nearest later sidereal time to local sidereal birth time (LSBT)				4 Convert to
3 Nearest earlier time to LSBT				seconds
4 Subtract answer for step 3 from answer for step 2				(A)
5 LSBT				7 Convert to
6 Nearest earlier time LSBT				seconds
7 Subtract answer for step 6 from answer for step 5				(B)
from Midheaven column 10 in Table of Houses	deg	mins	sign	
8 Midheaven for nearest later sidereal time		00		
9 Midheaven for nearest earlier sidereal time		00		
10 Subtract answer for step 9 from answer for step 8	1°	always		60 mins (C)
from Ascendant column in Table of Houses				
11 Ascendant for nearest later sidereal time				13 Convert to
12 Ascendant for nearest earlier sidereal time				minutes
13 Subtract answer for step 12 from answer for step 11				(D)

Comments: Remember to reverse signs for Southern Latitudes.

③ Now find and enter the *nearest earlier* sidereal time, for the same location.

④ Subtract the two and convert your answer from minutes and seconds to seconds only. This is your answer (A).

⑤ Now enter your local sidereal birth time (step 10 of the worksheet on page 24).

⑥ Enter your earlier sidereal time from your table of houses and step 3.

⑦ Subtract and convert your answer to seconds. Enter this as your answer (B).

⑧ The column headed "10" in your table of houses gives the midheaven for each sidereal time. Enter the corresponding placing for your later sidereal time, including the zodiac sign.

⑨ Repeat for your earlier sidereal time.

⑩ Subtract the two. Since the "10" column is already laid out in increments of one degree, your answer will always be the same. This is your answer (C).

⑪ Repeat for the later degree of your ascendant, from the "Ascendant" column in your table of houses, remembering again to write in the zodiac sign.

⑫ Enter your earlier ascendant degree.

⑬ Subtract and convert your answer to minutes. This is your answer (D).

SOUTHERN HEMISPHERE CONVERSION

If you were born in the southern hemisphere, take the polarity sign from that given in the table of houses for both your step 8 and step 11 figures. A table of sign polarities is given on page 43. For example, if the table of houses gives you a Pisces midheaven, keep the same number of degrees and minutes but it is Virgo (the sign opposite Pisces in the zodiac) that you should enter. Similarly, if you find that Cancer is given as your ascendant, your real rising sign will be Capricorn (the sign opposite Cancer in the zodiac). Astrology has its roots in the northern hemisphere, so this stage only applies if you were born in Australasia, southern Africa, South America and similar. If you were born in the northern hemisphere, you can skip this stage.

HOUSES FOR LONDON

Sidereal time			10 ♓	Ascendant ♋
Hours	Mins	Secs	Degrees°	Degrees°
22	34	54	7°	10°16
22	38	40	8°	11°02

HOLLY'S CALCULATIONS

WORKSHEET 3

① Nearest latitude to birthplace	**51** degrees	**32** minutes		
	hours	**mins**	**secs**	
② Nearest later sidereal time to local sidereal birth time (LSBT)	**22**	**38**	**40**	④ Convert to
③ Nearest earlier time to LSBT	**22**	**34**	**54**	seconds
④ Subtract answer for step 3 from answer for step 2		**3**	**46**	**226** (A)
⑤ LSBT	**22**	**38**	**11**	⑦ Convert to
⑥ Nearest earlier time LSBT	**22**	**34**	**54**	seconds
⑦ Subtract answer for step 6 from answer for step 5		**3**	**17**	**197** (B)
from Midheaven column 10 in Table of Houses	**deg**	**mins**	**sign**	
⑧ Midheaven for nearest later sidereal time	**8**	00	♓	
⑨ Midheaven for nearest earlier sidereal time	**7**	00	♓	
⑩ Subtract answer for step 9 from answer for step 8	**1°**	always		60 mins (C)
from Ascendant column in Table of Houses				
⑪ Ascendant for nearest later sidereal time	**11**	**02**	♋	⑬ Convert to
⑫ Ascendant for nearest earlier sidereal time	**10**	**16**	♋	minutes
⑬ Subtract answer for step 12 from answer for step 11		**46**		**46** (D)

Comments: Remember to reverse signs for Southern Latitudes.

STAGE 4: DETERMINE THE POSITION OF YOUR ASCENDANT AND MIDHEAVEN

Stage 4 is where you pinpoint the position of your ascendant and midheaven, which can then be plotted directly onto your birth chart. You're getting there!

TIME AND SPACE

There is no difference between entering degrees, minutes and seconds or hours, minutes and seconds on your calculator:

• 1 degree = 60 minutes
• 1 hour = 60 minutes

For the purposes of this exercise the two can be multiplied and divided interchangeably, since you are interested in the proportion of time and distance that has either elapsed or been traveled.

YOU WILL NEED
• scientific calculator
• answers A, B, C and D from worksheet 3 on page 26

WORKSHEET 4

Natal midheaven				
❶ Multiply answer B by answer C				
❷ Divide answer to step 1 by answer A				mins
❸ Add answer to step 2 to answer to step 9 in worksheet 3	deg	min	sign	
Natal ascendant				
❹ Multiply answer B by answer D				
❺ Divide answer to step 4 by answer A				mins
❻ Add answer to step 5 to answer to step 12 in worksheet 3	deg	min	sign	

NATAL MIDHEAVEN

1 Using your answers from worksheet 3, multiply your answer B by your answer C, treating these as ordinary numbers when entering them on your calculator.

2 Divide your answer by figure A from worksheet 3, again treating everything as a straightforward sum. Round off your answer to the nearest whole number.

3 Add this answer *as minutes* to your earlier midheaven (your answer to step 9 of worksheet 3). This is your natal midheaven.

NATAL ASCENDANT

4 Now, using your answers from worksheet 3, multiply your answer B by your answer D, treating these as ordinary numbers when entering them on your calculator.

5 Divide your answer by figure A, once more rounding your answer either up or down to the nearest whole number.

6 Add your answer *as minutes* to your earlier ascendant (your answer to step 12 of worksheet 3). This is your natal ascendant and can be written on your chart.

Well done, you have completed the most difficult part of calculating your own horoscope. The planets are next on your list!

HOLLY'S CALCULATIONS

WORKSHEET 4

Natal midheaven			
1 Multiply answer B by answer C		11,820	
2 Divide answer to step 1 by answer A in worksheet 3		52 mins	

	deg	min	sign
3 Add answer to step 2 to answer to step 9 in worksheet 3	7	52	♓

Natal ascendant			
4 Multiply answer B by answer D		9,062	
5 Divide answer to step 4 by answer A		40 mins	

	deg	min	sign
6 Add answer to step 5 to answer to step 12 in worksheet 3	10	56	♋

STAGE 5: LUMINARIES

You have now calculated the angles of your birth chart and the orientation of your horoscope. At the moment you still have to work out where your planets lie, so start by finding the Sun and Moon.

YOU WILL NEED

- scientific calculator
- midnight ephemeris

SUN AND MOON

1 Using your ephemeris, find the positions of the Sun and Moon on the day *after* your birthday. Note these down as Position 1 for each one. Follow Holly's example if you get confused!

2 Next find the position of the Sun and Moon on the day of your birthday. Note these down as Position 2.

3 Subtract Position 2 from Position 1 to tell you how far each planet moved on the day you were born. Write in your answer as the Daily (24hr) Motion of each planet.

You may find the Sun and Moon placings are given very precisely in your ephemeris, but you are safe rounding off these figures to the nearest minute.

WORKSHEET 5

Planet Longitudes						Planetary movement	Planet positions				
Position 1 = day after birth position Position 2 = birthday position						**4** GMT birth time =	Add (subtract retrograde) the planet's movements from midnight to birth time (answer to step 5) to the planet's birthday position				
		deg	min	sign	R$_X$			deg	min	sign	R$_X$
☉	**1** Position 1						**6** Sun birthday position				
	2 Position 2					**5** Daily Motion ÷ 24 x GMT birth time	**7** Add (subtract) planetary movement				
	3 Daily motion (position 1– position 2)					deg mins	**8** Sun birth time position				
☽	**1** Position 1						**6** Moon birthday position				
	2 Position 2					**5** Daily Motion ÷ 24 x GMT birth time	**7** Planetary movement				
	3 Daily motion (position 1– position 2)					deg mins	**8** Moon birth time position				

The Sun moves about one degree per day and circuits the zodiac in one year. The Moon circuits the zodiac in one month, moves on average 12½° every day and passes through each sign in roughly 2½ days. Because it moves so quickly, the Moon is quite likely to change sign during 24 hours, as it did on Christmas Eve 1931, the day that Holly was born. Thus if your Position 1 figure looks smaller than your Position 2, remember that 30 degrees of the sign in which the Moon was first placed have passed before the Moon entered the constellation in which it was later found.

PLANETARY MOVEMENT

④ Enter your GMT birth time (your answer to step 4 on worksheet 1).

⑤ Using your scientific calculator, enter your daily motion (your answer to step 3). Divide it by 24 and multiply your answer by your GMT birth time. Write in your answer as degrees and minutes, rounding off to the nearest minute as before. Do this for the Sun and then repeat for the Moon.

PLANET POSITIONS

⑥ Note down Position 2 as the birthday position.

⑦ Note down your Planetary Movement (your answer to step 5).

⑧ Add the two together to give the exact position for your birth time.

If your total goes over 30 degrees, then you have entered the next sign. The Sun and Moon are never retrograde, so you will only ever need to add. Retrograde means literally "stepping backward" and affects all the other planets from time to time. See page 33 to discover more.

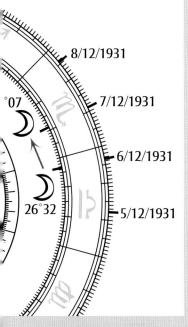

8/12/1931
°07
7/12/1931
6/12/1931
26°32
5/12/1931

Lunar motion is on average 12½° per day. Sometimes, like here, it can be more. It is easy for the Moon to change its sign during a 24 hour period.

HOLLY'S CALCULATIONS

WORKSHEET 5

Planet Longitudes						Planetary movement	Planet positions				
Position 1 = day after birth position Position 2 = birthday position						④ GMT birth time = 16:30	Add (subtract retrograde) the planet's movements from midnight to birth time (answer to step 5) to the planet's birthday position				
			deg	min	sign	Rₓ			deg	min	sign Rₓ
☉	❶ Position 1		2	14	♐		❻ Sun birthday position		1	13	♐
	❷ Position 2		1	13	♐		❺ Daily Motion − 24 x GMT birth time	❼ Add (subtract) planetary movement	0	42	
	❸ Daily motion (position 1– position 2)		1	01			0 deg 42 mins	❽ Sun birth time position	1	55	♐
☽	❶ Position 1		2	32	♋			❻ Moon birthday position		19	32	♊
	❷ Position 2		19	32	♊		❺ Daily Motion − 24 x GMT birth time	❼ Add (subtract) planetary movement	8	56	
	❸ Daily motion (position 1– position 2)		13	00			8 deg 56 mins	❽ Moon birth time position	28	28	♊

STAGE 6: PERSONAL PLANETS

Mercury, Venus and Mars move comparatively quickly and can be in different positions among individuals born relatively close together.

YOU WILL NEED
- scientific calculator
- midnight ephemeris

MERCURY, VENUS AND MARS

Calculating the personal planets follows the same format as for the luminaries (see worksheet 5 on pages 30–31).

However, with these and other planetary features, you will start to encounter a phenomenon known as retrogradation. This is marked in your ephemeris with an Rx symbol.

WORKSHEET 6

Planet Longitudes		deg	min	sign	Rx	Planetary movement	Planet positions		deg	min	sign	Rx
Position 1 = day after birth position Position 2 = birthday position						④ GMT birth time =	Add (subtract retrograde) the planet's movements from midnight to birth time (answer to step 5) to the planet's birthday position					
☿	① Position 1						⑥ Mercury birthday position					
	② Position 2					⑤ Daily Motion ÷ 24 x GMT birth time	⑦ Add (subtract) planetary movement					
	③ Daily motion (position 1– position 2)					deg mins	⑧ Mercury birth time position					
♀	① Position 1						⑥ Venus birthday position					
	② Position 2					⑤ Daily Motion ÷ 24 x GMT birth time	⑦ Planetary movement					
	③ Daily motion (position 1– position 2)					deg mins	⑧ Venus birth time position					
♂	① Position 1						⑥ Mars birthday position					
	② Position 2					⑤ Daily Motion ÷ 24 x GMT birth time	⑦ Planetary movement					
	③ Daily motion (position 1– position 2)					deg mins	⑧ Mars birth time position					

CREATING YOUR BIRTH CHART

RETROGRADE

Astrology looks at the heavens from the Earth. In reality, the Earth and the planets are all traveling in space, as they continue their orbits around the Sun.

Because this situation is dynamic, the faster-moving planets sometimes overtake us, or we will overtake a planet that is moving more slowly. In either case this temporarily makes that planet seem to move backward in the sky, even though this is only an optical illusion caused by our own perspective.

Mercury and Venus travel more quickly than the Earth, since they are nearer the Sun and have less far to go.

Mars, Jupiter, Saturn, Uranus, Neptune and Pluto all have orbits outside of the Earth, move more slowly and will thus be overtaken from time to time.

RECORDING RETROGRADES

Show a retrograde planet by putting an Rx symbol next to the planetary placing. Retrogradation can be important, so many ephemerides will highlight a retrograde period, but otherwise look for the Rx symbol when the cycle begins and for a D (direct) symbol when the planet moves forward again.

When a planet is in retrograde motion, your Position 2 will be greater than your Position 1 figure, without any sign change having taken place. Subtracting these two gives you a negative daily motion, a minus answer that should be taken away during Step 6.

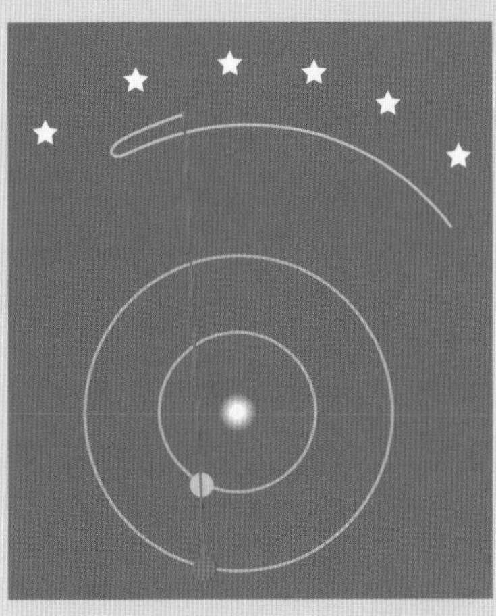

The retrograde cycle of Mercury and Venus, viewed from the Earth.

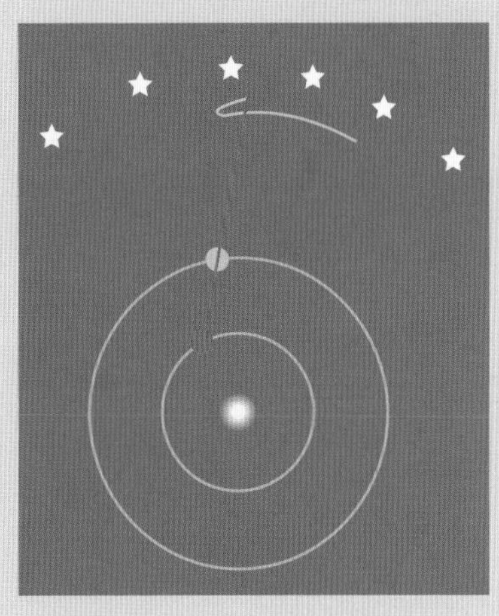

The retrograde cycle of all the other planets, viewed from the same perspective.

HOLLY'S CALCULATIONS

Holly was born with Mercury retrograde in the constellation of Sagittarius. Mercury moved 1°11 backward on the day of her birth, or just 0°49 between midnight and the time she was born. Subtracting this figure from the placing at midnight on her birthday gives Mercury's exact position for her birth time, highlighted with an Rx symbol on the worksheet.

WORKSHEET 6

Planet Longitudes						Planetary movement	Planet positions				
Position 1 = day after birth position Position 2 = birthday position						❹ GMT birth time = 16:30	Add (subtract retrograde) the planet's movements from midnight to birth time (answer to step 5) to the planet's birthday position				
		deg	min	sign	℞			deg	min	sign	℞
☿	❶ Position 1	23	53	♐	℞		❺ Mercury birthday position	25	04	♐	℞
	❷ Position 2	25	04	♐	℞	❺ Daily Motion ÷ 24 x GMT birth time	❻ Add (subtract) planetary movement	0	49		
	❸ Daily motion (position 1– position 2)	1	11			0 deg 49 mins	❼ Mercury birth time position	24	15	♐	℞
♀	❶ Position 1	28	59	♑			❺ Venus birthday position	27	44	♑	
	❷ Position 2	27	44	♑		❺ Daily Motion ÷ 24 x GMT birth time	❻ Add (subtract) planetary movement	0	52		
	❸ Daily motion (position 1– position 2)	1	15			0 deg 52 mins	❼ Venus birth time position	28	36	♑	
♂	❶ Position 1	11	21	♑			❺ Mars birthday position	10	35	♑	
	❷ Position 2	10	35	♑		❺ Daily Motion ÷ 24 x GMT birth time	❻ Add (subtract) planetary movement	0	32		
	❸ Daily motion (position 1– position 2)	0	46			0 deg 32 mins	❼ Mars birth time position	11	07	♑	

WORKSHEET 7

Planet Longitudes						Planetary movement	Planet positions					
Position 1 = day after birth position Position 2 = birthday position						**4** GMT birth time =	Add (subtract retrograde) the planet's movements from midnight to birth time (answer to step 5) to the planet's birthday position					
		deg	min	sign	R$_X$				deg	min	sign	R$_X$
2f	**1** Position 1						**6** Jupiter birthday position					
	2 Position 2					**5** Daily Motion ÷ 24 x GMT birth time	**7** Add (subtract) planetary movement					
	3 Daily motion (position 1– position 2)					deg mins	**8** Jupiter birth time position					
♄	**1** Position 1						**6** Saturn birthday position					
	2 Position 2					**5** Daily Motion ÷ 24 x GMT birth time	**7** Add (subtract) planetary movement					
	3 Daily motion (position 1– position 2)					deg mins	**8** Saturn birth time position					
♅	**1** Position 1						**6** Uranus birthday position					
	2 Position 2					**5** Daily Motion ÷ 24 x GMT birth time	**7** Add (subtract) planetary movement					
	3 Daily motion (position 1– position 2)					deg mins	**8** Uranus birth time position					
♆	**1** Position 1						**6** Neptune birthday position					
	2 Position 2					**5** Daily Motion ÷ 24 x GMT birth time	**7** Add (subtract) planetary movement					
	3 Daily motion (position 1– position 2)					deg mins	**8** Neptune birth time position					
♇	**1** Position 1						**6** Pluto birthday position					
	2 Position 2					**5** Daily Motion ÷ 24 x GMT birth time	**7** Add (subtract) planetary movement					
	3 Daily motion (position 1– position 2)					deg mins	**8** Pluto birth time position					

STAGE 7: SOCIAL AND OUTER PLANETS

In stage 7 you'll calculate the position of the social planets (Jupiter and Saturn) and the outer planets (Uranus, Neptune and Pluto).

YOU WILL NEED
- scientific calculator
- midnight ephemeris

JUPITER, SATURN, URANUS, NEPTUNE AND PLUTO

The method for calculating the positions of these planets is the same as for the luminaries (see worksheet 5 on pages 30–31).

SLOW MOTION

The motion of the outer planets is often extremely slow. The further a planet is from the Sun, the further it has to travel and the slower its motion becomes. On a daily basis you may not notice the outer planets moving very much at all. All of the outer planets spend a lot of time retrograde, as the Earth overtakes them again and again. Often they are almost stationary, when for some days, with some planets, they may appear barely to move at all.

As a result, the main difficulty when calculating their positions will be in dealing with such small movements. Remember that your conversion factor in Step 5 cannot possibly exceed your daily motion in Step 3. Round any stray seconds either up or down to the nearest minute.

HOLLY'S CALCULATIONS

An interesting calculation scenario in Holly's chart involves the planet Uranus, which while retrograde on her birthday turns direct the day after. Since Uranus started moving forward the day *after* Holly was born, it must still have been retrograde throughout her actual day of birth. A good ephemeris will tell you that Uranus resumed direct motion on December 25 at 15:11 GMT, so definitely must have been retrograde on the day she was born.

WORKSHEET 7

		Planet Longitudes	deg	min	sign	Rₓ		Planetary movement	Planet positions		deg	min	sign	Rₓ
		Position 1 = day after birth position Position 2 = birthday position					④	GMT birth time = **16:30**	Add (subtract retrograde) the planet's movements from midnight to birth time (answer to step 5) to the planet's birthday position					
♃	❶ Position 1		22	15	♌	Rₓ			❻ Jupiter birthday position		22	18	♌	Rₓ
	❷ Position 2		22	18	♌	Rₓ	❺	Daily Motion – 24 x GMT birth time	❼ Add (subtract) planetary movement		0	02		
	❸ Daily motion (position 1– position 2)		0	03				0 deg 02 mins	❽ Jupiter birth time position		22	16	♌	Rₓ
♄	❶ Position 1		22	57	♑				❻ Saturn birthday position		22	50	♑	
	❷ Position 2		22	50	♑		❺	Daily Motion – 24 x GMT birth time	❼ Add (subtract) planetary movement		0	05		
	❸ Daily motion (position 1– position 2)		0	07				0 deg 05 mins	❽ Saturn birth time position		22	55	♑	
♅	❶ Position 1		15	26	♈	Rₓ			❻ Uranus birthday position		15	26	♈	Rₓ
	❷ Position 2		15	26	♈	Rₓ	❺	Daily Motion – 24 x GMT birth time	❼ Add (subtract) planetary movement		0	00		
	❸ Daily motion (position 1– position 2)		0	00				0 deg 00 mins	❽ Uranus birth time position		15	26	♈	Rₓ
♆	❶ Position 1		7	56	♍	Rₓ			❻ Neptune birthday position		7	56	♍	Rₓ
	❷ Position 2		7	56	♍	Rₓ	❺	Daily Motion – 24 x GMT birth time	❼ Add (subtract) planetary movement		0	00		
	❸ Daily motion (position 1– position 2)		0	00				0 deg 00 mins	❽ Neptune birth time position		7	56	♍	Rₓ
♇	❶ Position 1		21	26	♋	Rₓ			❻ Pluto birthday position		21	28	♋	Rₓ
	❷ Position 2		21	28	♋	Rₓ	❺	Daily Motion – 24 x GMT birth time	❼ Add (subtract) planetary movement		0	01		
	❸ Daily motion (position 1– position 2)		0	02				0 deg 01 mins	❽ Pluto birth time position		21	27	♋	Rₓ

STAGE 8: CALCULATE THE MOON'S NODE AND CHIRON

In stage 8 you'll calculate the position of the Moon's north node and Chiron.

YOU WILL NEED

- scientific calculator
- midnight ephemeris

THE MOON'S NORTH NODE

You do this in the same way as you did for all of the planets and can follow Holly's example here.

MOON'S NODES

Two important factors in birth chart interpretation are the Moon's nodes, which represent the points of intersection between the orbit of the Earth around the Sun and of the Moon around the Earth.

We'll discuss their interpretation in Chapter 6, but for now try thinking of each planetary orbit as a hula hoop. In your mind's eye hold one hula hoop horizontal while putting the other one inside it at a slight angle. You will notice that the hoops are touching in two places and these, in cosmic terms, are your lunar nodes. The orbit of the Moon is angled to our own by just over five degrees. The point where the Moon rises above the Earth's orbit is termed the north or ascending node and the point where it slips back beneath our orbit again is termed the south or descending node. In zodiacal terms the north and south nodes are always directly opposite in the zodiac, so only the north node has to be calculated.

NORTH NODE— MEAN OR TRUE?

Unfortunately those worthy people who compile ephemerides have two theoretical approaches to calculating the nodal position: one that tries to take account of irregularities in the lunar orbit and one that is simpler and just averages things out.

Confusingly, the former is known as the *true node* and the latter is called the *mean node*, even though neither can be argued with certainty to have greater validity. The mean node is certainly much easier to use and is always retrograde, moving three to four minutes backward through the zodiac every day. This permanent retrogradation is caused by perturbations in the complex

WORKSHEET 8

Planet Longitudes		deg	min	sign	R$_x$	Planetary movement	Planet positions		deg	min	sign	R$_x$
Position 1 = day after birth position Position 2 = birthday position						④ GMT birth time =	Add (subtract retrograde) the planet's movements from midnight to birth time (answer to step 5) to the planet's birthday position					
	① Position 1						⑥ North node birthday position					
☊	② Position 2					⑤ Daily Motion ÷ 24 x GMT birth time	⑦ Add (subtract) planetary movement					
	③ Daily motion (position 1– position 2)					deg mins	⑧ North node birth time position					

dynamics of the lunar orbit. Its constant nature means that the Rx symbol can safely be omitted from your worksheet.

Having two alternative ways to measure the lunar nodes makes life confusing, but in reality the differences between them are very small. The mean lunar node has been used here for clarity, although you may need to hunt around for an ephemeris that provides sufficient detail. The American Ephemeris gives the true node on a daily basis and the mean node once a month. The World Ephemeris for 2001–2050, published by Astrolabe, gives mean *daily* nodal placings, as does its forerunner for the 20th century, published by Para Research.

CHIRON

Chiron is a recent addition and was only discovered in 1977. It is believed once to have been a comet, now trapped in the outer solar system, orbiting continuously between Saturn and Uranus. Chiron is thought to embody, from an astrological perspective, some of the qualities connected with both.

We discuss Chiron's interpretation during Chapter 6, but for now it's worth noting that at only about 106 miles (170 km) across, Chiron is diminutive in celestial terms. Despite this, it has been observed to have a powerful impact, so include Chiron in your birth charts if you can.

Ephemerides for the 21st century usually include Chiron, but older editions often only give a monthly placing, if that. The latest Astrolabe ephemeris has the advantage of listing Chiron's position every day, but otherwise a software-based solution may be your only option, at least for 20th-century births.

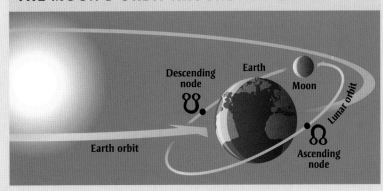

THE MOON'S ORBIT AROUND THE EARTH

Descending node ☊

Earth

Moon

Earth orbit

Lunar orbit

Ascending node ☋

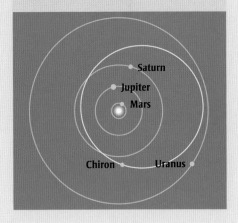

CHIRON'S PLACE IN OUR SOLAR SYSTEM

Saturn

Jupiter

Mars

Chiron

Uranus

HOLLY'S CALCULATIONS

WORKSHEET 8

Planet longtitudes						Planetary movement	Planet positions				
Position 1 = day after birth position Position 2 = birthday position						**4** GMT birth time = *16:30*	Add (subtract retrograde) the planet's movements from midnight to birth time (answer to step 5) to the planet's birthday position				
			deg	min	sign	Rx			deg	min	sign	Rx
	1 Position 1		0	39	♈	Rx	**6** North node birthday position	0	42	♈	Rx
☊	**2** Position 2		0	42	♈	Rx	**5** Daily Motion – 24 x GMT birth time	**7** Add (subtract) planetary movement	0	02		
	3 Daily (24 hour) motion (position 1– position 2)		0	03			0 deg 02 mins	**8** North node birth time position	0	40	♈	Rx

STAGE 9: THE PART OF FORTUNE

The Part of Fortune is one of the so-called Arabic parts, a series of points calculated to give more information on specific themes within an individual horoscope, based on the distinctive combination of planets, angles and sometimes other factors in the unique birth chart concerned.

THE ARABIC PARTS

Such factors were popular among Arabian astrologers around the turn of the first millennium, hence the reference in their name. It seems that things may have grown a little out of hand, though, since nearly a hundred were at one time recorded, ranging from the intriguing Part of Life or Part of Marriage, through to the less immediately engrossing Part of Beans or the Part of Melons, Lemons, Cucumbers and Gourds. Mention of the Part of Fortune stretches back even further than this, though, to the time of Ptolemy of Alexandria in the 2nd century AD and probably to long before. It is the only Arabic part still widely used and we'll look at its interpretative significance in Chapter 6.

THE FORMULA

The Part of Fortune is worked out using a formula involving three of the most crucial factors in your birth chart—your Sun, Moon and ascendant. These are combined together using this formula to show a point that, for you, is a likely indicator of great joy, happiness and personal fulfillment.

moon + asc - sun = pof

ABSOLUTE LONGITUDE

Some astrologers believe that the formula for the Part of Fortune should vary depending on whether you were born at night or during the day. It is safer to use the same formula throughout, though, since this helps to eliminate doubt and confusion.

First convert each of these placings into absolute longitude, a measurement of their position in the zodiac that bypasses the 12 signs. Absolute longitude starts at zero degrees and keeps counting once you hit 30. One degree of Taurus is 31 degrees of absolute longitude, so 5° Gemini 00 is 65° AL 00 and 21° Scorpio 53 becomes 231° AL 53, since the number of minutes is unaffected by your conversion. Pisces ends at 359° AL 59 and it is back to zero degrees in both systems. You can refer to the diagram below for a shortcut to where all of the different signs begin.

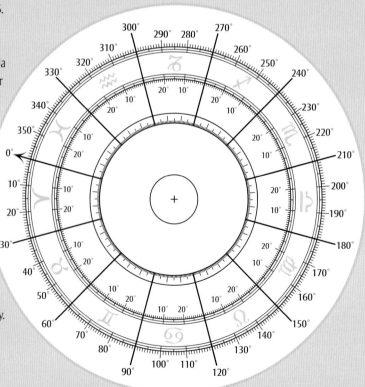

YOU WILL NEED

• scientific calculator

CALCULATE THE PART OF FORTUNE

1 Note down your Moon birth time position (see worksheet 5).

2 Convert to absolute longitude (AL).

3 Note down your ascendant position (see worksheet 4).

4 Convert to absolute longitude (AL).

5 Note down your Sun birth time position (see worksheet 5).

6 Convert to absolute longitude (AL).

7 Add together the Moon and ascendant placings using your scientific calculator and make a note of your answer. Remember, there are sixty minutes in one degree.

8 If the Sun's placing is too large to subtract from your total, you should add in 360°00 to enable you to do so, but only if necessary. Similarly, if your final answer exceeds 360°00, you should subtract this figure to conclude.

9 Convert your answer to step 8 back to the natural zodiac to obtain your Part of Fortune.

WORKSHEET 9

	deg	min	sign
1 Moon birth time position			
2 Convert answer to step 1 to AL			
3 Ascendant position			
4 Convert answer to step 3 to AL			
5 Sun birth time position			
6 Convert answer to step 5 to AL			
7 Add answer to step 2 to answer to step 4			
8 Subtract answer to step 6 from answer to step 7 (add 360°00 to step 7 if necessary)			
9 Convert to natural zodiac position (subtract 360°00 if necessary)			

HOLLY'S CALCULATIONS

WORKSHEET 9

	deg	min	sign
1 Moon birth time position	28	28	♊
2 Convert answer to step 1 to AL	88	28	AL
3 Ascendant position	10	56	♋
4 Convert answer to step 3 to AL	100	56	AL
5 Sun birth time position	01	55	♑
6 Convert answer to step 5 to AL	271	55	AL
7 Add answer to step 2 to answer to step 4	189	24	AL
8 Subtract answer to step 6 from answer to step 7 (add 360°00 to step 7 if necessary)	277	29	AL
9 Convert to natural zodiac position (subtract 360°00 if necessary)	7	29	♑

CHAPTER

2

DRAW YOUR BIRTH CHART

GETTING STARTED

Now you are ready to draw up your birth chart. Photocopy the blank birth chart template from page 7 onto good quality or colored paper for a special impact.

Your birth chart is a symbolic view of the sky from the Earth. Imagine standing outside in an open space on a dark night. Notice how the sky above your head resembles a dome. This is shown in two dimensions by the top half of your birth chart. As the Earth revolves in space, the planets continue their journey beneath us too, rising in the east and setting in the west, day after day and year after year. The circular pattern of the birth chart is a representation of the zodiac transcribed by the planets across the sky.

Using your figures from the worksheets in Chapter One you can now

• complete the zodiac and draw in your angles (see pages 42–43)

• define your house system and plot your planets (see pages 44–45)

• measure and record your aspects, where planets influence one another to modify their effects (see pages 46–49)

• analyze your elemental balance (see pages 50–51)

• understand all the other data that your birth chart contains (see pages 52–55)

Each step of the process is illustrated with Holly's example chart, which will enable you to see exactly how the process works.

YOU WILL NEED

• pencil
• ruler
• eraser
• Wade's Wheel (see page 46)

. . . and you are ready to go. Although not essential, the following would also prove useful:

• colored pens or pencils for effect
• compasses for drawing circles
• correcting fluid for that occasional mistake

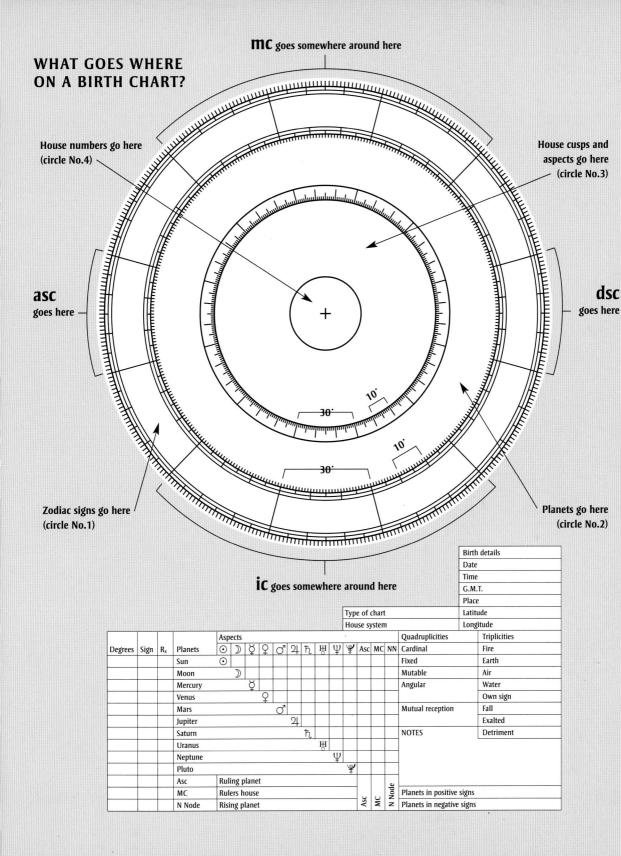

WHAT GOES WHERE ON A BIRTH CHART?

mc goes somewhere around here

House numbers go here
(circle No.4)

House cusps and
aspects go here
(circle No.3)

asc goes here

dsc goes here

30° 10° 10° 30°

Zodiac signs go here
(circle No.1)

Planets go here
(circle No.2)

ic goes somewhere around here

				Aspects																	Quadruplicities		Triplicities
Degrees	Sign	Rx	Planets	☉	☽	☿	♀	♂	♃	♄	♅	♆	♇	Asc	MC	NN		Cardinal		Fire
			Sun	☉														Fixed		Earth
			Moon		☽													Mutable		Air
			Mercury			☿												Angular		Water
			Venus				♀													Own sign
			Mars					♂										Mutual reception		Fall
			Jupiter						♃											Exalted
			Saturn							♄								NOTES		Detriment
			Uranus								♅									
			Neptune									♆								
			Pluto										♇							
			Asc	Ruling planet																
			MC	Rulers house											Asc	MC	N Node	Planets in positive signs		
			N Node	Rising planet														Planets in negative signs		

Birth details	
Date	
Time	
G.M.T.	
Place	
Type of chart	Latitude
House system	Longitude

HOLLY'S CHART

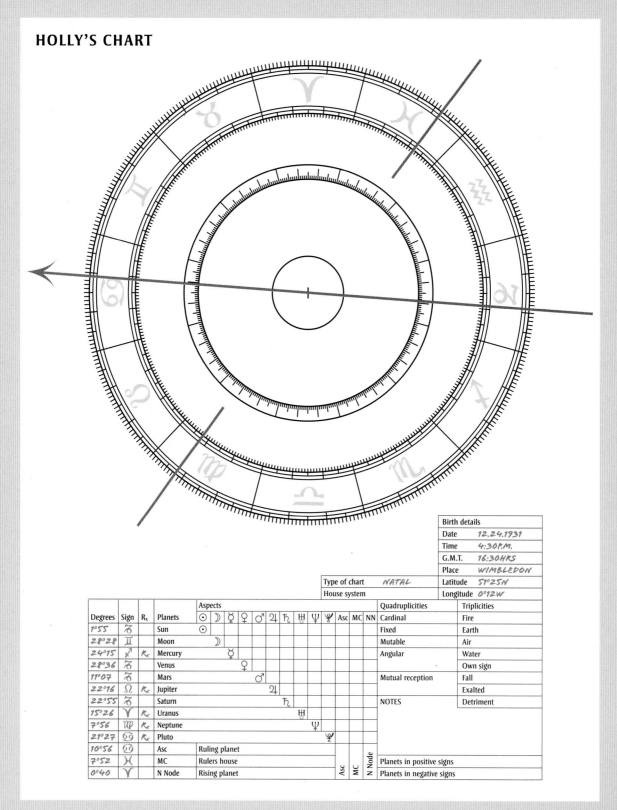

Birth details	
Date	12.24.1931
Time	4:30P.M.
G.M.T.	16:30HRS
Place	WIMBLEDON

Type of chart	NATAL	Latitude	51°25N
House system		Longitude	0°12W

Degrees	Sign	Rx	Planets	Aspects												Asc	MC	NN	Quadruplicities		Triplicities
				⊙	☽	☿	♀	♂	♃	♄	♅	♆	♇					Cardinal		Fire
1°55	♑		Sun	⊙														Fixed		Earth
28°28	♊		Moon		☽													Mutable		Air
24°15	♐	Rx	Mercury			☿												Angular		Water
28°36	♑		Venus				♀													Own sign
11°07	♑		Mars					♂										Mutual reception		Fall
22°16	♌	Rx	Jupiter						♃											Exalted
22°55	♑		Saturn							♄								NOTES		Detriment
15°26	♈	Rx	Uranus								♅									
7°56	♍	Rx	Neptune									♆								
21°27	♋	Rx	Pluto										♇							
10°56	♋		Asc	Ruling planet																
7°52	♓		MC	Rulers house										Asc	MC	N Node	Planets in positive signs		
0°40	♈		N Node	Rising planet													Planets in negative signs		

ANGLES AND SIGNS

1 Write your calculated placings from Stages 1–9 in Chapter 1 into the left-hand column of your aspects table. Write in degrees, minutes and the sign position, together with a retrograde symbol if necessary. The mean lunar node is always retrograde, so you don't really need to record it as such. Here we are working with Holly's placings, but you should work on your own, perhaps in pencil to begin.

2 Put your birth details into the box at the right of your chart template. Put the date, local time and place of your birth, together with your GMT corrected time and your birth latitude and longitude. Record that this is a natal, or birth chart, where shown.

3 Draw the glyph for your ascending sign in the extreme left-hand section of your birth chart's outer wheel. This circle represents the zodiac and is divided into 12 signs. Place the polarity (opposite) sign from your ascendant in the extreme right-hand section of this circle.

4 Complete your zodiac circle, which, once it concludes with Pisces, starts from the beginning with Aries again. You will note that the order of the signs runs counterclockwise, with Gemini preceding Cancer, which in turn precedes Leo, for example.

5 Because the zodiac is a circle, it is made up of 360 degrees. Because there are 12 signs, each one comprises 30 degrees. On your template each sign is divided into ten- and five-degree subsections, with an individual mark for every degree. Remember always to count counterclockwise from the preceding sign.

6 Make a mark showing the position of your ascendant as accurately as you can: 30 minutes is about half a degree, 45 minutes is about three-quarters. Accuracy is important, since you will be using these points for measurement later, but don't beat yourself up about it.

7 Make a mark at a point opposite your ascendant, at the same number of degrees and minutes but in the polarity sign. Join these two points with a continuous straight line passing exactly through the center of your chart.

8 This is your ascendant/descendant axis, the horizon for this instant. Your descendant constellation was setting in the west, opposite your ascendant that was rising in the east. Putting an arrow on the left-hand side of this line helps your ascendant to stand out.

9 Repeat this process for your MC/IC axis, with the IC opposite the MC as before. Draw lines for these points as indicated, but don't put arrows on them or continue them across the chart. The MC is always toward the top of your horoscope, but because of complex celestial dynamics it can vary widely between the left- and right-hand sides. Draw it in wherever it has fallen for you.

10 You are now well on your way to constructing your own horoscope. The ascendant and midheaven, the descendant and the IC are described collectively as the four angles of the birth chart.

POLARITY SIGNS

aries	<–>	libra
taurus	<–>	scorpio
gemini	<–>	sagittarius
cancer	<–>	capricorn
leo	<–>	aquarius
virgo	<–>	pisces

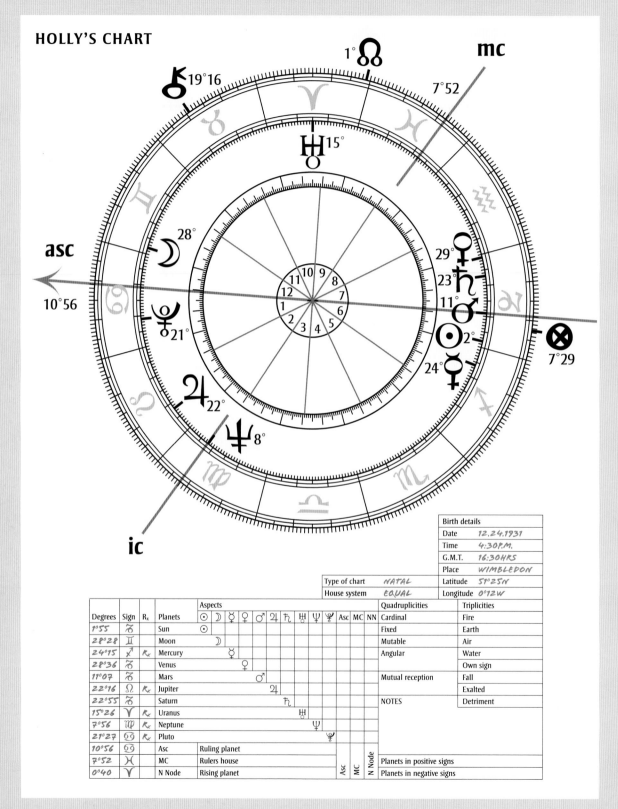

HOLLY'S CHART

Birth details	
Date	12.24.1931
Time	4:30 P.M.
G.M.T.	16:30 HRS
Place	WIMBLEDON

Type of chart	NATAL	Latitude	51°25N
House system	EQUAL	Longitude	0°12W

Degrees	Sign	Rx	Planets	Aspects										Asc	MC	NN	Quadruplicities	Triplicities
				☉	☽	☿	♀	♂	♃	♄	♅	♆	♇				Cardinal	Fire
1°55	♑		Sun	☉													Fixed	Earth
28°28	♊		Moon		☽												Mutable	Air
24°15	♐	Rx	Mercury			☿											Angular	Water
28°36	♑		Venus				♀											Own sign
11°07	♑		Mars					♂									Mutual reception	Fall
22°16	♌	Rx	Jupiter						♃									Exalted
22°55	♑		Saturn							♄							NOTES	Detriment
15°26	♈	Rx	Uranus								♅							
7°56	♍	Rx	Neptune									♆						
21°27	♋	Rx	Pluto										♇					
10°56	♋		Asc	Ruling planet														
7°52	♓		MC	Rulers house										Asc	MC	N Node	Planets in positive signs	
0°40	♈		N Node	Rising planet													Planets in negative signs	

DEFINE YOUR HOUSE SYSTEM

The astrological houses are a symbolic division of your birth chart into 12, corresponding with the natural sign divisions of the zodiac. There are several different ways to achieve this division, but one of the oldest, most popular and most effective methods is known as Equal House. Reassuringly, it is also the only method that doesn't require any further calculation.

1 Write Equal in the box marked House System under Type of Chart.

2 Make a series of marks on the inside of the central measuring circle (Circle 3), with each one advancing from the ascendant by thirty degrees.

For example, Holly's ascendant is at 10°56 Cancer. Note that thirty degrees onward from this is 10°56 Leo, followed by 10°56 Virgo, 10°56 Libra and so on. Because each sign is also thirty degrees, the start of each subsequent house is at the same position, but in the adjacent sign.

3 Continue marking these points right around your chart. The cusp, or beginning, of the Seventh House is already signified by your descendant. The ascendant is the cusp of your First House.

4 Once complete, join up these sets of opposite points so that each connecting line passes exactly through the center of your chart. Extend these lines only to the inside edges of your measuring circle.

5 Moving counterclockwise from your ascendant, number your houses 1–12 inclusive, writing these numbers in the innermost circle (Circle 4), with the First House just beneath your ascendant and the Twelfth House just above. Take a breather, your house system is complete!

PLOT YOUR PLANETS

When you are ready, plot your planets on the inside of your zodiac circle (Circle 2). Sometimes you will need to space out their glyphs in the interests of clarity, but do make a precise and visible mark for each one, since you will be using it for measurement later. Also, do make it obvious which point corresponds with which glyph.

1 Write the nearest number of whole degrees next to each planet, rounding up for 30 minutes or more and down for anything less.

2 Don't do this with a placing like 29°43, though, where rounding up would take you incorrectly into the next sign. In cases such as this, you will need to make room for your minutes too.

MARK OTHER FEATURES

The north node, Chiron and the Part of Fortune are drawn in the same way, but around the outside of your chart. Where there is nowhere to mark their full degree placing elsewhere, it is a good idea to write this next to the appropriate glyph.

1 Label your ascendant and MC as illustrated, with their full placing.

2 Label your IC and start thinking about your aspects . . .

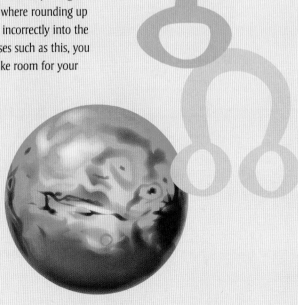

MEASURE YOUR ASPECTS

Measuring your aspects might seem daunting. All those curious lines and patterns in the center of the chart and all of those symbols in your aspects table, where do you begin?

WADE'S WHEEL

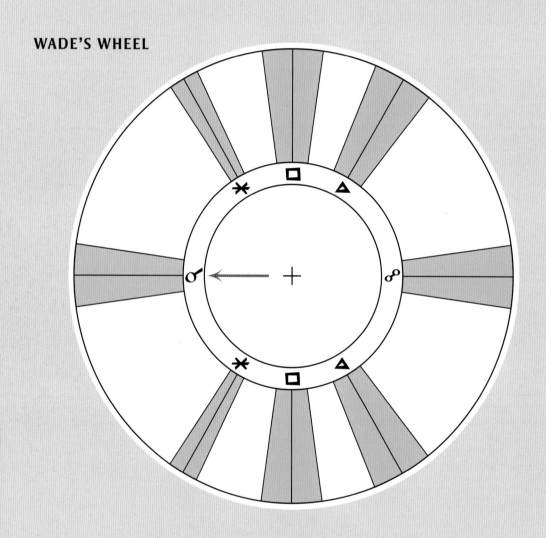

This process isn't so hard, but you will need a little help, in the form of your Wade's Wheel, the instant aspect finder detailed opposite. Photocopy this onto laser transparency, a kind of transparent plastic that will stand up to this sort of thing. These transparencies cost a little more than paper, but are the same size, are used in the same way and should be widely available. Ensure that the laser component is defined specifically before attempting to make your copy, since cheaper plastics will melt inside your machine, possibly causing irreparable damage.

You only need to record your five major aspects. For each of these an *orb of influence* is allowed either side of exactitude, within which the aspect is considered still to be in effect. These orbs are illustrated by the shaded areas on either side of each exact aspect line on your Wade's Wheel. By placing your transparent aspect finder on top of your birth chart and by lining it up with each planet at a time, you are able to read off all of the aspects to that planet, and from right around the birth chart, all at once.

HOW TO MEASURE YOUR ASPECTS

1. Take your transparent Wade's Wheel and place it over your chart, lining up the center of the aspect finder with the center of your birth chart and the central line of the exact conjunction with the mark you made earlier, showing the exact position of the planet you are checking out.

2. You can spin your aspect finder around and even use it upside down, but you should never turn it over, or it will not work properly. Upside down writing on your Wade's Wheel is fine, back to front mirror writing is not. You might like to pin both chart and wheel through the center to a cork board, which can make reading off your aspects even faster.

3. Once properly aligned to the mark of the planet you are assessing, it is easy to see those planets and other chart features that are within allowable orbs of this point. Note these down on a separate piece of paper, ready to put on your aspects table at the next stage.

4. Start by measuring aspects to your Sun, then continue with the Moon, Mercury, Venus, Mars and so on. Remember to include the angles, north node, Chiron and the Part of Fortune in your aspect measurements.

THE MAJOR ASPECTS

	aspect	relationship	orb
♂	conjunction	0° apart	+/– 8°00
✳	sextile	60° apart	+/– 4°00
□	square	90° apart	+/– 8°00
△	trine	120° apart	+/– 8°00
☍	opposition	180° apart	+/– 8°00

THE MINOR ASPECTS

	aspect	relationship	orb
⚻	inconjunct	150° apart	+/– 2°00
⚺	semi-sextile	30° apart	+/– 2°00
∠	semi-square	45° apart	+/– 2°00
⚼	sesquiquadrate	135° apart	+/– 2°00
Q	quintile	72° apart	+/– 2°00
BQ	biquintile	144° apart	+/– 2°00

RECORD YOUR ASPECTS

Once you have recorded your aspects, it is time to start writing them on your aspects table. The aspects table is at the bottom left of your birth chart template and is divided into rows running across and columns running down.

HOW TO RECORD YOUR ASPECTS

1 When two planets are in aspect, put the symbol for the aspect they form, where the row of one planet intersects with the column of the other in your aspects table. As you move down the table, there are fewer possible aspects to consider. While you must record the relationship of the Sun to everything else and the Moon to all but the Sun, by the time you reach Pluto there are only the angles and the node to go.

2 Now, make a point corresponding with each planet on your chart wheel itself, somewhere inside Circle 3, a little way in from your measuring circle. To get all your points equidistant, you can draw a fine circle in pencil with a compass, make your points and then rub out the circle later. These points will not be used for measuring, so you can spread them out for clarity, being sure that where you have a stellium, or cluster, of planets close together, it is clear which point belongs to which one. Once you have finished you should have ten points, since you are noting the ten planets only. Count them to be sure!

3 Aspects are drawn in the center of the birth chart using straight lines of different kinds. Aspects involving the angles, node, Chiron or the Part of Fortune are omitted, so only those connecting two planets need to be recorded here. Conjunctions are usually clear, so aren't drawn either.

You can tell which aspect is being made by the type of line that is used. Both squares and oppositions use a heavy double thickness line, but you can readily distinguish between the two, since opposition lines always pass roughly through the center of your chart. Some people prefer to use color (see below), but remember that if you ever need to take a black and white photocopy of your horoscope, it probably will be unreadable.

4 Draw in your aspect lines and watch the patterns build. These will be fully interpreted in Chapter 4. Don't worry about aspect lines crossing or overlapping, because this is all a part of the picture. Wherever two planets are recorded as in aspect in your aspects table, connect the points for those two planets in the center of your chart, with the correct type of line for the aspect concerned. By the time you have finished, the wheel of your birth chart is complete!

ASPECT LINES

aspect	line	color
☌ conjunction	not drawn	not needed
✳ sextile	- - - - -	blue
☐ square	——————	red
△ trine	——————	green
☊ opposition	——————	purple

48

HOLLY'S CHART

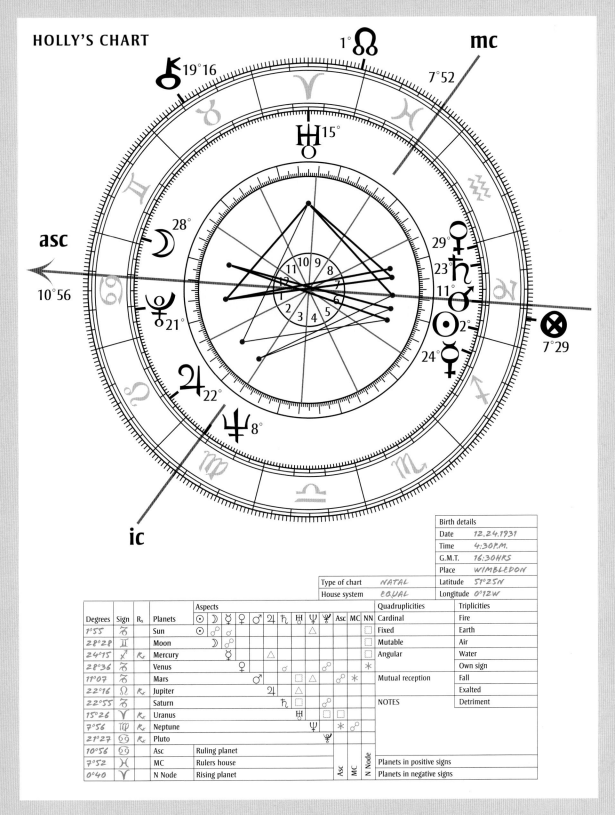

mc — 1° ♌ / 7°52
asc — 10°56
ic

19°16 — Uranus ♅ 15° — Venus ♀ 29° / Saturn ♄ 23° / Mars ♂ 11° / Sun ☉ 2° / Mercury ☿ 24° / ⊗ 7°29
Moon ☽ 28° / Pluto ♇ 21° / Jupiter ♃ 22° / Neptune ♆ 8°

Birth details	
Date	12.24.1931
Time	4:30P.M.
G.M.T.	16:30HRS
Place	WIMBLEDON

Type of chart	NATAL	Latitude	51°25N
House system	EQUAL	Longitude	0°12W

Degrees	Sign	Rx	Planets	Aspects ☉	☽	☿	♀	♂	♃	♄	♅	♆	♇	Asc	MC	NN	Quadruplicities	Triplicities
1°55	♑		Sun	☉	☍	☌					△					□	Cardinal	Fire
28°28	♊		Moon		☽							☍					Fixed	Earth
24°15	♐	Rx	Mercury			☿			△							□	Mutable	Air
28°36	♑		Venus				♀	♂			☍				*	Angular	Water
11°07	♑		Mars					♂	□	△	☍		*				Own sign
22°16	♌	Rx	Jupiter						♃	△						Mutual reception	Fall
22°55	♑		Saturn							♄	□	☍					Exalted
15°26	♈	Rx	Uranus								♅	□	□		NOTES	Detriment
7°56	♍	Rx	Neptune									♆	*	☍		
21°27	♋	Rx	Pluto										♇		
10°56	♋		Asc	Ruling planet												Planets in positive signs
7°52	♓		MC	Rulers house								Asc	MC	N Node		
0°40	♈		N Node	Rising planet												Planets in negative signs

ELEMENTS AND QUALITIES

The 12 signs are categorized in three ways, depending on characteristics they share. These classifications are element, secta and quality.

ELEMENT

Elements are also referred to as triplicities because each element has three members.

Fire (action) You're dynamic, enthusiastic, positive and energetic, with an optimistic and lively approach.

Earth (practicality) You are practical, cautious and methodical, a conservative person who sees the importance of the material world.

Air (intellect) You are communicative and friendly, with an intellectual inclination and a logical perspective.

Water (emotion) You are intuitive, sensitive and emotional. You might be psychic and are always very deep.

SECTA

The elements themselves can also be categorized by shared features.

Positive signs (self-expressive) Fire and air signs are together termed positive, active or masculine, on account of their fundamentally self-expressive nature.

Negative signs (self-repressive) Earth and water signs are together termed negative, receptive or feminine signs, since they tend usually toward greater self-containment.

TRIPLICITIES AND QUADRUPLICITIES

triplicity (element)	quadruplicity (quality)		
	cardinal	fixed	mutable
Fire	Aries	Leo	Sagittarius
Earth	Capricorn	Taurus	Virgo
Air	Libra	Aquarius	Gemini
Water	Cancer	Scorpio	Pisces

QUALITY

The signs are also classified another way, by their quality or quadruplicity, so-called because each has four members, all linked according to their basic approach.

Cardinal (initiator) You are active, vigorous and enterprising, with ambition, courage and the ability to lead.

Fixed (organizer) You are steadfast, intense, determined and stubborn. You aren't easily swayed from your chosen course.

Mutable (communicator) You are versatile, adaptable and multifaceted, with a talent for spreading the word.

This gives one cardinal, one fixed and one mutable member of each element and a unique pattern that does not repeat.

RECORDING YOUR ELEMENTS AND QUALITIES

1 On a piece of paper, note how many of your planets are found in the signs of each element.

2 Repeat, but note this time how many planets fall in signs belonging to each quality.

3 Record your totals where indicated on your chart.

4 Since you are concerned with the planets only, check that both your totals add up to ten!

5 Add together your answers for Fire and Air to give the number of planets in positive signs.

6 Repeat for Earth and Water to give the number of planets in negative signs.

HOLLY'S CHART

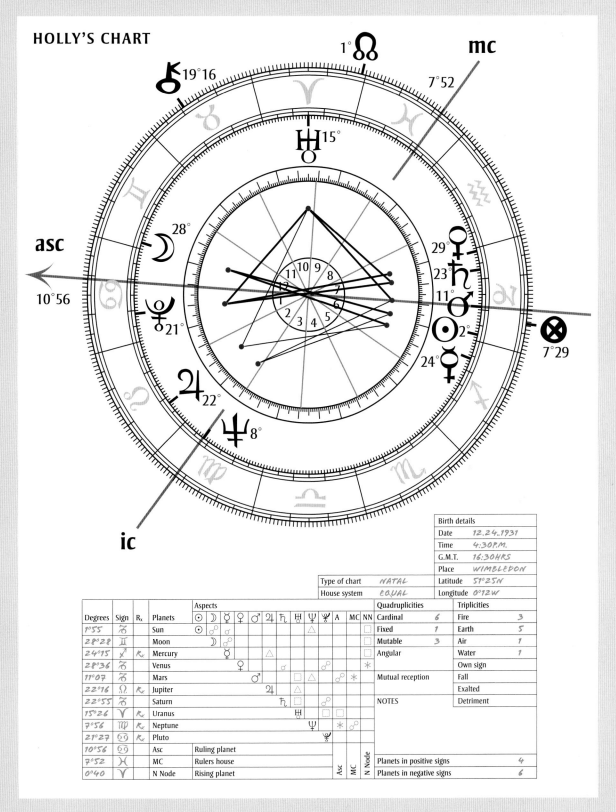

asc 10°56

mc 7°52

ic

Birth details	
Date	12.24.1931
Time	4:30 P.M.
G.M.T.	16:30 HRS
Place	WIMBLEDON

Type of chart	NATAL	Latitude	51°25N
House system	EQUAL	Longitude	0°12W

Degrees	Sign	Rx	Planets	Aspects											A	MC	NN	Quadruplicities		Triplicities	
				⊙	☽	☿	♀	♂	♃	♄	♅	♆	♇				Cardinal	6	Fire	3
1°55	♑		Sun	⊙	⚹	♂			△							☐	Fixed	1	Earth	5
28°28	♊		Moon		☽	⚹										☐	Mutable	3	Air	1
24°15	♐	Rx	Mercury			☿										☐	Angular		Water	1
28°36	♑		Venus				♀		☐			⚹							Own sign	
11°07	♑		Mars		♂			♂	☐	△		♂	⚹				Mutual reception		Fall	
22°16	♌	Rx	Jupiter					△	♃										Exalted	
22°55	♑		Saturn							♄	☐		♂				NOTES		Detriment	
15°26	♈	Rx	Uranus								♅	☐	☐							
7°56	♍	Rx	Neptune									♆	⚹	♂						
21°27	♋	Rx	Pluto										♇							
10°56	♋		Asc	Ruling planet																	
7°52	♓		MC	Rulers house								Asc	MC	N Node		Planets in positive signs		4		
0°40	♈		N Node	Rising planet												Planets in negative signs		6		

51

NOTABLE PLACINGS

Continuing to analyze the data in your horoscope, you should next work out those planets that are strongly placed and those that by their sign position might face trickier circumstances.

DIGNITY (OWN SIGN)

Each planet has a sign it traditionally rules, with the characteristics of that planet in special harmony with the traits of that sign. For example, Jupiter is linked with good fortune, so rules Sagittarius, the luckiest sign. Since there are twelve signs and ten planets, there are two planets that rule two signs each, with Mercury ruling Gemini and Virgo and Venus ruling Taurus and Libra. If a planet is found in the sign that it rules, it is said to be in dignity, or in its *own sign*,

DETRIMENT

If a planet is found opposite its own sign in your horoscope it is termed in *detriment*, a weaker placing for that planet but not necessarily a bad one for you. For example, the Sun rules Leo, since the Sun is connected with ego, and those born under this constellation have a strong sense of self. The Sun is in detriment in Aquarius, since this sign is more concerned with group dynamics. Mercury and Venus have two rulerships and two detriment placings.

EXALTATION

Exaltation placings are strong, although maybe not so favorable as a dignity. These associations have been

THE PLANETS AND THEIR NOTABLE PLACINGS

planet	own sign	exaltation	detriment	fall
Sun	Leo	Aries	Aquarius	Libra
Moon	Cancer	Taurus	Capricorn	Scorpio
Mercury	Gemini and Virgo	Aquarius	Sagittarius and Pisces	Leo
Venus	Taurus and Libra	Pisces	Aries and Scorpio	Virgo
Mars	Aries	Capricorn	Libra	Cancer
Jupiter	Sagittarius	Cancer	Gemini	Capricorn
Saturn	Capricorn	Libra	Cancer	Aries
Uranus	Aquarius	Scorpio	Leo	Taurus
Neptune	Pisces	Aquarius	Virgo	Leo
Pluto	Scorpio	Leo	Taurus	Aquarius

determined over time, with some linking the oldest to celestial observations made in 786 BC! Many exaltations do make sense, though, if you think about the archetypes they portray. For example, the Sun's exaltation in Aries shows a pure, joyful and uncomplicated expression of the self. The Moon's exaltation in Taurus confers deep, steady and stable emotions. What better sort are there?

FALL

The fall position is opposite the exaltation in zodiacal terms. It is seen as an awkward placing, but again, in

personal terms, maybe not that bad for you. The Sun is fall in Libra, for example, since Libra is of all constellations the most concerned with partnership. This does not mean that Sun in Libra is a bad placing for the individual, when some more forceful energies might actually benefit from a softer approach.

IN YOUR CHART

Take a look at this table. Wherever in your horoscope you find a planet in one of these positions, note down its glyph in the appropriate box on your birth chart template.

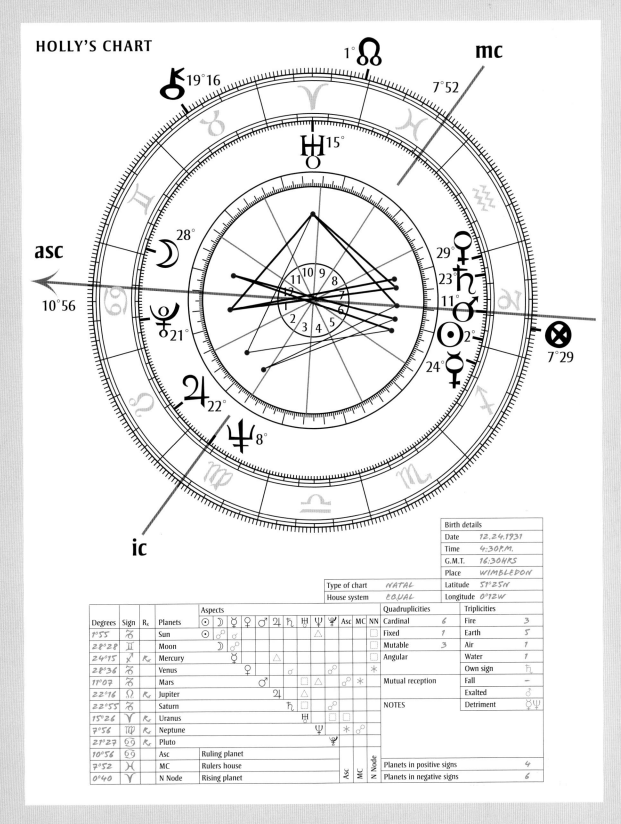

HOLLY'S CHART

asc · mc · ic

Birth details

Date	12.24.1931
Time	4:30 P.M.
G.M.T.	16:30 HRS
Place	WIMBLEDON

Type of chart	NATAL	Latitude	51°25N
House system	EQUAL	Longitude	0°12W

Degrees	Sign	Rx	Planets	Aspects ☉	☽	☿	♀	♂	♃	♄	♅	♆	♇	Asc	MC	NN	Quadruplicities		Triplicities	
1°55	♑		Sun	☉	☍	♂			△								Cardinal	6	Fire	3
28°28	♊		Moon		☽	☍											Fixed	1	Earth	5
24°15	♐	Rx	Mercury			☿	△										Mutable	3	Air	1
28°36	♑		Venus				♀	♂		☍					*		Angular		Water	1
11°07	♑		Mars					♂	□	△	☍	*							Own sign	♄
22°16	♌	Rx	Jupiter						♃	△		☍					Mutual reception		Fall	–
22°55	♑		Saturn						♄	□	☍								Exalted	♂
15°26	♈	Rx	Uranus							♅	□	□				NOTES		Detriment	☿♆
7°56	♍	Rx	Neptune							♆	*	☍								
21°27	♋	Rx	Pluto							♇										
10°56	♋		Asc	Ruling planet																
7°52	♓		MC	Rulers house										Asc MC N Node			Planets in positive signs			4
0°40	♈		N Node	Rising planet													Planets in negative signs			6

OTHER FEATURES

You will be pleased to discover that your birth chart is now largely complete, with just a few details remaining. The knowledge you have acquired along the way will prove useful in their completion.

RULING PLANET

Your ruling planet is the one that rules your ascending sign. For example, with Virgo rising your ruling planet is Mercury, and with Cancer rising your ruling planet is the Moon. It doesn't matter whether your ascendant is early or late in the sign, it is the sign itself that you should note. Write the glyph for your ruling planet where indicated on your birth chart.

RULER'S HOUSE

The ruler's house is the house in your birth chart where your ruling planet is to be found. With Holly, her ruling planet is the Moon and it is found in her Twelfth House. Don't make the mistake of putting the Fourth House here, just because that is the one with which the Moon is usually linked.

RISING PLANET

Your rising planet is the one closest to your ascendant, so long as it is within eight degrees. This means that if you don't have a planet conjunct with your ascendant, you don't have a rising planet in your chart. It is only possible to have one rising planet, so should more than one be within this range, then only the closest to your ascendant ought to be selected. If two planets are exactly the same distance away, then the faster moving is your choice. Conjunctions can occur from either the First House or the Twelfth House, with a broadly similar impact, more visible in the first case.

ANGULAR PLANETS

Angular planets are those conjunct with an angle—the ascendant, descendant, midheaven or IC. The only exception is your rising planet if you have one, which having been noted as rising need not be noted again. You can have one angular planet, none or several. Record those you have in the box provided.

MUTUAL RECEPTION

Mutual reception brings two planets into a beneficial relationship, even if no aspect exists between them. It occurs when two planets swap rulership, according to their position in your chart. Say, for example, you have Mars in Sagittarius and Jupiter in Aries. This is a mutual reception of Mars and Jupiter, since Mars rules Aries and Jupiter rules Sagittarius. There is a natural affinity between these two placings in your horoscope.

Another example is Sun in Scorpio and Pluto in Leo, where again, according to their rulerships, the natural position of these planets has been switched around. The placing of Mercury in Aquarius could be matched with Uranus in either Gemini or Virgo, because of the double rulership of Mercury. Venus can be considered in a similar way.

Unfortunately there is no shortcut for spotting your mutual receptions. Start with the Sun and work your way through, checking for a corresponding placing each time. Note each pair of planets in the box provided, or make a dash if nothing is found. Not every chart will have a mutual reception. Some have one, a few have two and on rare occasions you might even discover three.

NOTES

By completing your notes section with the aspects to Chiron and your Part of Fortune, you have now joined that select group who can both calculate and draw a birth chart.

You will undoubtedly have gained great insight into astrological technique, planetary dynamics and your own capabilities along the way. With your new understanding, you are ready to begin a similar approach to birth chart interpretation.

HOLLY'S CHART

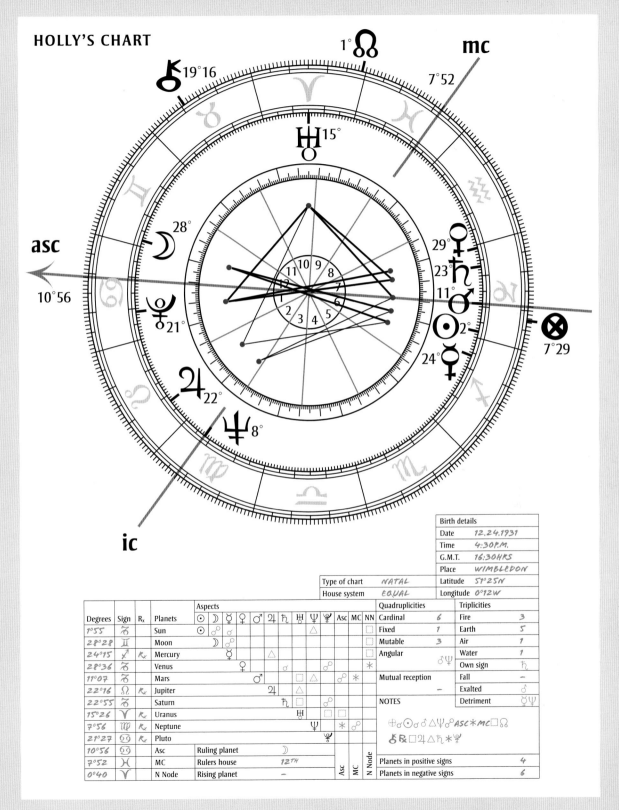

asc 10°56

mc 7°52

ic

Birth details

Date	12.24.1931
Time	4:30 P.M.
G.M.T.	16:30 HRS
Place	WIMBLEDON

Type of chart	NATAL	Latitude	51°25N
House system	EQUAL	Longitude	0°12W

Degrees	Sign	Rx	Planets	Aspects ☉ ☽ ☿ ♀ ♂ ♃ ♄ ♅ ♆ ♇ Asc MC NN	Quadruplicities		Triplicities	
7°55	♑		Sun	☉ ☍ ☌ △	Cardinal	6	Fire	3
28°28	♊		Moon	☽ ☍	Fixed	1	Earth	5
24°15	♐	Rx	Mercury	☿ △	Mutable	3	Air	1
28°36	♑		Venus	♀ ☌ ☍ ✳	Angular		Water	1
11°07	♑		Mars	♂ □ △ ☍ ✳		♂♆	Own sign	♄
22°16	♌	Rx	Jupiter	♃ △	Mutual reception		Fall	–
22°55	♑		Saturn	♄ □ ☍		–	Exalted	♂
15°26	♈	Rx	Uranus	♅ □ □	NOTES		Detriment	☿♆
7°56	♍	Rx	Neptune	♆ ✳ ☍	♀☌☉♂△♆☍ASC✳MC□☊			
21°27	♋	Rx	Pluto	♇	♂Rx□♃△♄✳♆			
10°56	♋		Asc	Ruling planet ☽				
7°52	♓		MC	Rulers house 12TH			Planets in positive signs	4
0°40	♈		N Node	Rising planet –		Asc MC N Node	Planets in negative signs	6

UNDERSTANDING YOUR BIRTH CHART

Interpreting the birth chart is a three-stage process. You can plod through, starting with the Sun and ending with Pluto, assessing every house, sign and aspect position along the way. You will get good results, but your progress will be less than inspired and you may not consider some important factors until later than they deserve. By contrast, follow a few flexible interpretation guidelines and you'll soon be picking out the most vital features in the order of their importance. You will then have a much better idea of how these disparate factors all fit together. Stick closely to your guidelines initially, but in time you can adapt these to your own needs.

INTERPRETATION ESSENTIALS

HOW TO INTERPRET YOUR CHART

Astrological interpretation is another world. Like your DNA, a birth chart delineation is a complex thing, one that is unique to you and shows you how you really are. But the same DNA that makes us each so different from one another always comprises the same four molecules, and it is only the differences in the way these components are put together that make us each so separate and distinct.

A birth chart interpretation is a similar concept, with an end result that is as complex and unique as you are, but which is made up of four much simpler components. In astrological terms these components are:

- the houses

- the signs

- the planets and angles

- the aspects

There is much more about synthesizing your interpretations during Chapter 4 and beyond, but for now we'll look at the importance of establishing firm principles, which cannot be underestimated. Everything you need to analyze and understand your own astrological birth chart is easily accessible over the next few pages.

You should start by thinking about the houses where an energy is manifest and the signs that show you how that energy is expressed. The planets and angles will show you which energy is under consideration in the first place, while the aspects will demonstrate how effectively that energy is integrated with the rest of your chart.

HOUSES

Drawn in the center of your birth chart, the 12 houses correspond to 12 areas of your life, with the whole of human experience contained within their reach. Planets placed in a house impart their planetary energy to this area, for good or for less so, depending on the combination. The symbolism and associations of each house are described concisely in the pages that follow, with ideas to get you thinking about what each planet means when it's found there.

SIGNS

The zodiac sign in which a planet is placed shows how the energy of that planet will be manifesting. Each sign defines a particular way of being and behaving, so any planet found within a certain constellation will express itself in the manner connected with that sign. No sign is better than any other and there are eight favorable and eight more challenging traits listed under each one. Then, you have brief notes on every planet's impact in every sign, to get your burgeoning interpretations well under way.

PLANETS

Planets express themselves in the area of life shown by their house placing and in the manner of the sign in which they are found. Each planet shows a different part of your personality, since ultimately we are all multifaceted. The symbolism of every planet is explained, together with some firm ideas on how each can work either favorably or less well in your chart.

ANGLES

Just as important as the planets, the ascendant/descendant and MC/IC axes provide crucial information about your interaction with other people, your closest relationships, your emotional expectations, your domestic situation and where you are going with your life. There are brief delineations to get you thinking about every combination of both axes.

ASPECTS

Aspects modify the impact of the planets connected. They help to highlight your strengths and pinpoint your dilemmas, showing where energies combine helpfully or less so within your chart, and where they complement one another or might be causing conflict, at least until you get to understand yourself as fully as you can.

Since there are so many different possible combinations, you'll be guided through a framework for understanding the different energies at work. This is much better than trying to remember detailed interpretations for each one, and besides, this way you'll have something new to reveal on every occasion. In time, your interpretative skills should improve steadily, as you practice this formula for working out aspect meanings for yourself.

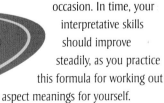

FIRST HOUSE

The First House is the first thing others notice about you. In a real house, it would be the front door. It shows your outer personality and the impression you give on first meeting.

YOUR PLANETS IN THE FIRST HOUSE

SUN
Your true character shines through. Your charisma makes it hard to walk into a room unnoticed. You could be confident and outgoing or more reserved and intense, depending on your Sun sign.

MOON
You don't hide your emotions. Happy or sad, you won't keep it to yourself. You have a natural empathy and are close to your mother. Your feelings vacillate, and you are prone to moods.

MERCURY
You love to talk, sing, write letters, send e-mails and call up your friends on your cell phone. You are easily bored and hate dull routines. You like lots of interesting things to do.

VENUS
Harmony is your thing. You like it when everybody gets along in pleasant surroundings. You hate arguments, so put up with too much rather than making a scene, even when you should.

MARS
You are an assertive person with, in most cases, lots of energy. You are forthright and upfront. You benefit from keeping busy, either in the world of work or, better still, through physical activity.

JUPITER
You are optimistic, enthusiastic, good-humored and tolerant. Often, you will love to travel. Some born with this placing are physically large; others just have a broad mind, a big heart and a gigantic personality.

SATURN
You take life seriously and can find it hard to have fun. Often you'll get greater satisfaction from attending to your work and to the duties and responsibilities you are always setting for yourself.

URANUS
You need freedom to breathe and to be yourself. You are unusual and there is something arresting about your appearance. You might dress distinctively and have a style that is very much your own.

NEPTUNE
You are creative and imaginative, with an artistic or musical inclination you may have yet to develop fully. You are sensitive to the thoughts and feelings of others, so appreciate a peaceful home life.

PLUTO
You are self-contained and secretive and have the original poker face. You are focused and determined and possess great strength of character. To perceptive individuals, your brooding intensity may be more apparent than you'd like.

SECOND HOUSE

How you spend money is an accurate reflection of what matters most to you and, therefore, your whole value system. This house deals with your employment options, money, worldly possessions and attitudes toward security.

YOUR PLANETS IN THE SECOND HOUSE

SUN

The material world is important to you, although you would rather accept less money than take a gamble with your essential security. You can be very possessive, both of people and things.

MOON

You have a need to feel safe and secure. This powerful impulse might not be apparent on a conscious level. You may wonder why material spoils prove less satisfying than you were expecting.

MERCURY

You are always alert to a moneymaking opportunity. Education, training and the development of your communication skills will prove profitable. You could do well in a career such as travel, transport, communications or publishing.

VENUS

Venus casts an auspicious light on your financial affairs. Although holding on to money has never been your greatest skill, there always seems to be enough when you need it. A well-heeled partner is ideal!

MARS

Fairly regularly in your life, sources of discord trace back to money. You put enormous effort into building your material security, yet are equally likely to blow everything on that one spontaneous purchase.

JUPITER

Easy come, easy go is your underlying ethos. Jupiter ensures that plentiful opportunities come your way, but what you make of these is largely up to you. A more steadying influence often proves helpful!

SATURN

Traditionally regarded as inauspicious, this placing was thought to confer poverty on those born under its sway. Often, though, this is not the case. You are prudent and focused enough to amass great wealth.

URANUS

Your finances are up and down. You have your own set of values and care more for personal freedom than you do for

material acquisition. You're suited for self-employment and enjoy working with new technology.

NEPTUNE

There is much potential for confusion in your financial affairs, with a need for you always to keep things clear and above board. Music, fashion, film and the arts could prove attractive employment options.

PLUTO

When it comes to money and possessions, you're the zodiac's ultimate control freak. You don't necessarily want to be the richest, but you do fear powerlessness. You want total control over your worldly affairs.

THIRD HOUSE

Ruled by Mercury, the Third House indicates your logical mind, conscious thought processes, your speech, how you write and other forms of communication. It has a strong link with education, your siblings and with your community involvements.

YOUR PLANETS IN THE THIRD HOUSE

SUN
You have above average intelligence and seek to prove yourself through intellectual accomplishment. You are a talented communicator, with literary skill and a flair for languages. Brothers and sisters feature prominently in your life.

MOON
Your logical mind and emotional nature are inextricably linked. This helps you to understand and talk about your feelings, but can make it difficult to gain a truly objective view.

MERCURY
You are always out and about. Probably you won't go far from home, but whether it's your car or any other form of transport that you choose, it is definitely your favorite thing.

VENUS
Your heart melts at the sound of sweet nothings. You need a loquacious partner with the gift of the gab. You probably met your significant other through the Lonely Hearts column in the local newspaper.

MARS
You have strong opinions about a number of things and don't intend to keep these to yourself. You get very upset if anybody questions your views and rather relish the idea of a good argument.

JUPITER
Life is a voyage, as with your endless philanthropy, tolerance and curiosity you seek to learn everything about this fascinating world. You might do this through formal education, or by traveling far away.

SATURN
You think your outlook is only realistic, but actually you're a pessimist. You have a strong sense of right and wrong, which is largely self-imposed and stems from experiences in your early days.

URANUS
Tradition is something you don't always respect. You'll be fine if you see good reason, but if people use this mainly as a method of control, they had better look out for the consequences.

NEPTUNE
You are creative, imaginative, artistic and could express your-self most effectively through music, dance or other non-verbal means. You have excellent intuition, but experience rather more difficulty putting your impressions into words.

PLUTO
You would make a great politician, because nobody will ever sway you. Your outlook changes irrevocably several times, but no one will ever force you.

FOURTH HOUSE

The Fourth House shows your home, both during childhood and in later life. It has a particular connection with the nurturing parent, not necessarily your biological mother, but whoever played that role for you.

YOUR PLANETS IN THE FOURTH HOUSE

SUN
You are a private person and the focus of your existence is your home. Your life improves from middle age. Your feelings and emotions are strong, but often you will keep them to yourself.

MOON
The relationship shared with your nurturing parent is a primary influence. You won't feel complete, either in childhood or later, without a supportive domestic and family situation, and as an adult you'll need a home to call your own.

MERCURY
You like keeping your mind active when at home. You could have quite a library, or an eclectic selection of glossy magazines. You are friendly with your neighbors and could be interested in genealogy.

VENUS
Some people like to go out a lot, but for you there's nothing like a cozy night in. If your home isn't tidy, attractive and comfortable, you could find yourself flustered and upset.

MARS
You need to keep busy around the house, since you have a lot of energy, which, unless constructively expended, often breaks out in arguments and discord. Home improvements could be something you'd enjoy!

JUPITER
Ideally you would like a large house, somewhere rambling and slightly decrepit in the countryside. You assist the development of those you love and do everything to help them reach their potential.

SATURN
Your home life could be a little cold. Probably you had a strict upbringing and experienced privation, especially in terms of emotional warmth. Now you're a doer, but find it harder to relate emotionally.

URANUS
Your home life is unusual. Perhaps you live on a houseboat or in a community run along progressive lines. You could have moved house a lot and have a knack for feeling comfortable anywhere.

NEPTUNE
You are very idealistic about your home and may need to realize that nowhere is that perfect. There were hidden circumstances surrounding your early environment. Ideally, you live in the countryside or beside water.

PLUTO
At home, you're the boss. You experienced a very controlling maternal figure and a home environment filled with guilt, manipulation and unspoken undercurrents. If you aren't careful, you will replicate this same situation for yourself.

FIFTH HOUSE

This house covers fun, holidays, hobbies, pets, recreation, sport and speculation. Creativity in the broadest sense, children as a creative act, and romance as a true expression of ourselves all find a place.

YOUR PLANETS IN THE FIFTH HOUSE

SUN

You are lost without opportunities for fun and romance. Your creative energies burn brightly and children will be an issue. You may love them to pieces, but could decide not to have any yourself.

MOON

Everybody needs to play sometimes. You will personally develop more as a result of your spare-time interests, which some might consider recreational, than through any amount of dull duty and obligation.

MERCURY

You have a good sense of humor and enjoy stretching your intellectual faculties. You love crosswords, quizzes and word games and articulate individuals who can entertain and make you laugh.

VENUS

Venus in the Fifth House needs romance. You are a sad individual if you have no love and laughter in your life. You are creative and, at the very least, always have an appreciation of beautiful things.

MARS

You are confident and assertive and admire the same traits in others. You are competitive and could be good at sports. It isn't the taking part you like, it is being there to win.

JUPITER

In your world, life is one great, long carnival. Your appetite for all kinds of sensory indulgence is both legendary and enormous, with a penchant for risk-taking that often seems to pay off.

SATURN

You're one of those people who enjoys working. Take you to a party and you're at a loss. Your best chance of romance is with a serious, mature person who appreciates the work ethic.

URANUS

You are either a wacky person, or seem normal and have wacky friends. You enjoy unusual hobbies such as extreme sports, you keep dangerous pets or you may be happier online with the latest computer game.

NEPTUNE

Romantically you are extremely idealistic. Your misty-eyed condition does not allow the object of your affections to appear clearly. Could this be your ideal mate, or have you just kissed another frog?

PLUTO

Victor or vanquished, the game isn't over until the opposition has been thoroughly annihilated and wiped from the face of the Earth. Playing to win doesn't even begin to describe it.

SIXTH HOUSE

The Sixth House shows your work, duties, obligations, responsibilities and the daily minutiae of your life. It is connected with your health, diet, your attitudes toward routine and how you feel about helping others.

YOUR PLANETS IN THE SIXTH HOUSE

SUN

Your happiness is linked directly with how useful you feel. Without purposeful activity you feel surplus to requirements and your health suffers. Health is always a minor obsession anyway.

MOON

You need to be involved with your work and, without this, could feel drained and apathetic. Given purpose you can work long and hard, but under less clear direction find it harder to focus.

MERCURY

You are good with routines and like an ordered environment. This placing has a special link with learned skills, with handicrafts, with hairdressing and with activities that require close coordination of the hand and eye.

VENUS

You are likely to meet your partner while at work, where generally you enjoy happy relationships with all your colleagues and subordinates. Alternatively, you might fall in love *with* your work . . .

MARS

You are industrious, have lots of enthusiasm and you love a challenge. You don't take kindly to overzealous supervision or to limitations in your agenda, so you are happiest working independently.

JUPITER

Theoretically you are fortunate, because your health and constitution are robust. Unfortunately, a tendency toward excess in most things, from working to eating and drinking, will serve over time to put this to the test.

SATURN

You work very hard and excel wherever sustained attention to detail is necessary. You take life seriously and can succumb to stress, so you must manage your responsibilities carefully.

URANUS

Self-employment has to be the best route for you. A safer second choice would be an autonomous position within a large organization, but only if you are able to set your own agenda.

NEPTUNE

You are extremely compassionate toward other people and like to help those who need it wherever you can. You are interested in nutrition and alternative forms of healing. You probably suffer from allergies.

PLUTO

You get very involved in your work. You need to be completely engrossed before you can tackle any task to the best of your abilities. If something doesn't grip you, you probably won't bother.

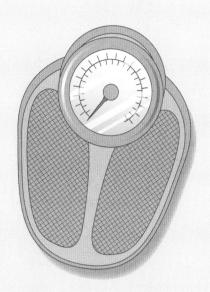

SEVENTH HOUSE

This house deals with your closest and most intimate relationships, those on a one-to-one basis and in a marriage or similar situation. Close professional associations, as well as more hostile and competitive links, are also indicated.

YOUR PLANETS IN THE SEVENTH HOUSE

SUN
You only really shine through that one special person. They must be confident and showy enough for you to admire, but not so bombastic and overbearing that your own spark is lost.

MOON
Close partnership for you is a tangible need. You only really feel complete once you have found that special person, although you may take some time discovering this is actually the truth.

MERCURY
You need a clever partner who entertains you with their stimulating repartee. You are a talker yourself and need good verbal and intellectual interaction with anyone you see more than once in a while.

VENUS
With the planet of love in the partnership house, an intimate relationship is essential. You need affection so much that you can keep silent when it is sometimes better just to clear the air.

MARS
You are fiery and provocative, especially when it comes to affairs of the heart. You are attracted to courage and bravery and need a partner who is not afraid to stand up to you.

JUPITER
You are easily bored. You like to feel life is going somewhere and this applies to your relationships too. You are particularly attracted to those of different ages, from different backgrounds and nationalities.

SATURN
Your attitude toward relationships is not light-hearted. As a result you are slow to get involved, but can stick with a difficult situation until the bitter end. You might even decide to stay single.

URANUS
Loose and unconventional attachments are the only kind that succeed. Close relationships last longest when there is something unusual about them, so don't be in too much of a hurry to tie things down.

NEPTUNE
Some might find it easy taking advantage of your compassionate and sympathetic nature. No sacrifice is too great for those you love, but unless you are very careful, you could end up getting hurt.

PLUTO
Relationships are a battleground for you and alter the course of your personal development more than anything else. Even the best seem fraught with power struggles and issues surrounding who is boss.

EIGHTH HOUSE

The Eighth House is connected with shared resources, other people's values and assorted financial dealings—including loans, insurance and tax. On a deeper level this house shows change, depth and complexity, including spiritual values far from the material world.

YOUR PLANETS IN THE EIGHTH HOUSE

SUN
You have experienced changes so complete that, when you look back, they seem almost to have happened to somebody else. These changes have not taken place easily, but ultimately have been for the best.

MOON
You need to experience true emotional and sexual intimacy. You are complex and emotionally deep. It will be important to share your life with another. Your emotions evolve in cycles.

MERCURY
You are a deep thinker and keep a lot to yourself. You find it hard to express your thoughts, but could be surprised at the sympathetic ear you'd receive if you did.

VENUS
Love for you is complicated, with much strategic planning, countless endgames, incredible subtleties of emphasis and many tests of nerve, determination and cunning. Others either love your approach—or hate it!

MARS
You have considerable entrepreneurial spirit, which would find constructive outlet in the business world. On a personal level you are jealous, possessive and territorial and have some lessons to learn about cooperative living.

JUPITER
You are lucky with money. Often others seem to help you through. Although you can find it hard holding on to your material reserves, help always seems to be there just when you need it.

SATURN
A major event has left you feeling that everything could change. Subconsciously you fear this, although sometimes change is an improvement. It is the only thing of which we can be sure.

URANUS
Major changes happen suddenly and with little warning. Often you are the secret catalyst. In a way you thrive on such extreme developments.

NEPTUNE
You might be described as psychic, since the impressions you form of people and places are both powerful and hard to ignore. To get the most from this, you'll need a firm grounding in material reality.

PLUTO
In times of crisis and of change, you are in your element. Where shared resources are concerned, it is best for everybody to know where they stand, since interference isn't something you welcome.

NINTH HOUSE

This house deals with thinking and ideas, and how they are applied as organized schemes of thought in wider society. Religion, philosophy, personal freedom and travel to broaden the mind all feature.

YOUR PLANETS IN THE NINTH HOUSE

SUN

You want to know more about the world in which we live. There are two main ways you can do this, through travel or through education. Either can help guide you toward broadened horizons.

MOON

It is likely with this placing that you will at some point live abroad. Many of your adult views were formed early, with your mother—or whoever played this role for you—exerting a major influence.

MERCURY

You could be interested in learning a foreign language. You try to be tolerant and dislike pettiness in every form. Although travel will certainly interest, the pull of further education could prove more enduring.

VENUS

You fall in love with someone of a different age, background, race or nationality. You meet them while abroad, or while studying at college. You could decide to teach and will adore your subject.

MARS

You have strongly held philosophical and religious principles, but probably don't see them in these terms. You just know what you believe to be right and will stand up for these things if necessary.

JUPITER

You have a faith that guides your life. Perhaps you have firm religious convictions. Education helps everybody, but is particularly advantageous for you. Expect growth experiences while traveling or connected with people from abroad.

SATURN

Your outlook is common-sense. An appreciation of propriety was instilled by your father figure. You prefer tried and tested routes to risky alternatives. You miss opportunities by being too cautious.

URANUS

Your views are distinctive, unusual and strongly held. You favor humanitarian and egalitarian philosophies, but believe also in rewarding the individual and those able to rise through their own efforts.

NEPTUNE

You have a compassionate outlook and a sensitive nature and are spiritually oriented. Your spiritual beliefs influence your world view enormously, but otherwise you embrace a broad spectrum of faiths, linked loosely by a mystical inclination.

PLUTO

You are often black and white about things and are very obstinate when it comes to altering your position in any way. Your views will change totally several times, although never as a result of external persuasion.

TENTH HOUSE

This house shows your place in society, your social status and the regard that others have for your achievements. It relates to your aims, to your worldly ambitions and often to your career aspirations.

YOUR PLANETS IN THE TENTH HOUSE

SUN
Your father, or equivalent paternal figure, has had a huge influence. You show unusual regard for those whose abilities and attainments you respect. In time, you will want to achieve similar for yourself.

MOON
Your ambitions have been influenced considerably by your parents and by the circumstances in which you grew up. You would do well working with the public, with property or land or with products for the home.

MERCURY
A communications career would suit. Depending on other placings, you could be anything from a writer, to a singer, to a telecommunications engineer, to a television presenter, plus lots of different possibilities in between.

VENUS
You want to marry your boss. You need to feel proud of your partner and love authority and status. Harmony is important, so you feel even minor problems keenly.

MARS
You are tireless in pursuit of your chosen objectives and take any question as a personal affront. You could either carve out a business empire for yourself, or waste your time fighting your superiors.

JUPITER
You are lucky where your career is concerned and in pursuit of your chosen objectives. You are fortunate in not having to try that hard, but still enjoy the best outcomes when you do.

SATURN
Much depends on your childhood experiences with authority. Either way, the world seems unforgiving and a struggle from the start. While some are encouraged to prove themselves, others perceive failure as their certain reward.

URANUS
One of your parents is individualistic, with a particular agenda and a direction all their own. You now have a hard act to follow, but it's an example that ideally you will strive to emulate.

NEPTUNE
You often feel confused about where you are heading. You might even consider personal ambition to be a deplorable characteristic. You could devote yourself to music, to charity or to furthering your creative interests.

PLUTO
You pursue your objectives zealously and with dedication, application and commitment. You are ruthless with those who try to block your way. Your life plan changes several times, as reflected outwardly in your career path.

ELEVENTH HOUSE

The Eleventh House relates to society, to friendship and to groups you interact with regularly. It illustrates your hopes and aspirations, on a more qualitative level than the aims and ambitions of the preceding house.

YOUR PLANETS IN THE ELEVENTH HOUSE

SUN

You express your individuality through the groups you join. By looking at your friends, you'll find out who you are. Relationships could be pleasant or more difficult, depending on other influences.

MOON

You are not a loner and much appreciate the company of your friends. You enjoy being among those with whom you share a common interest. Your own aspirations can fluctuate wildly in their intensity and focus.

MERCURY

Group interactions are important and you may have a special talent for getting your message across. You are an inspirational leader, or might favor a less public role—as the perfect group secretary, for example.

VENUS

Your friendships are close and warm. Throughout your life your friends are set to play a major role. You are generally popular and well-liked and have a talent for making others feel really special.

MARS

Ideally your friends are assertive and confident, since your own manner is abrasive at times. You are forever organizing some social event or get-together and could be active in team sports.

JUPITER

You naturally attract friends who are good for you. They make you happy, assist you in getting along and could help you out materially. You will always be ready to support them in return.

SATURN

You feel rather distant from others, unless you have some important duty to perform. As teacher, group leader or with another vital role to play, you can be relied upon to uphold your responsibilities.

URANUS

You are attracted to societies with advanced, progressive and esoteric interests. You might appear conventional, but your friends are much more unusual. You enjoy interacting online with special-interest groups and discussion forums.

NEPTUNE

You are sympathetic, kind and giving where your friends are concerned. Unfortunately they don't always return the favor, so you gradually learn better judgment about who is worth helping.

PLUTO

You are powerfully influenced by your friends and by the groups to which you belong. You admire strength, so are better with those who have a clear agenda and a constructive purpose.

TWELFTH HOUSE

This is the house of your subconscious, encompassing dreams, mysticism, intuition and self-sacrifice. Planets placed here can be both a hidden strength and a hidden weakness, depending largely on your appreciation of their effects.

YOUR PLANETS IN THE TWELFTH HOUSE

SUN

Entering this house shortly after sunrise, the Sun's rays are subdued and more muted. You are probably quite shy and keep yourself to yourself, or else develop a showy façade to hide behind.

MOON

You keep your feelings hidden, both from others and from yourself. You are warm and nurturing, but past hurts and upheavals have taught you rarely to reveal your inner self.

MERCURY

You may not have much to say. This doesn't mean there's nothing going on inside you, since there is plenty. Non-verbal methods might just be better for getting your message across.

VENUS

This placing is linked with impossible affairs and with unrequited love. Manifestations include secret liaisons, the love of a fan for their movie idol or a concealed attraction to somebody who never knows.

MARS

You work best on your own. When you have things to do, you will try to escape from the public gaze. Other people can discourage you, but you don't need their support to progress.

JUPITER

You are an optimist. No matter what happens, there is always something to cushion the fall. Much is down to your positive attitude. You expect things to succeed—and they usually do!

SATURN

Insecurity springs from your earliest days, so you are keen to make your life steady and permanent. You succeed with logic and planning and with self-control, but should try not to judge yourself harshly.

URANUS

Inside you, there is an individual bursting to get out. Your earliest experiences did not encourage you to express your true potential. So what is holding you back now, do you think, except yourself?

NEPTUNE

Neptune is the planet of compassion, found here in the house that it rules. You are sensitive, caring, empathetic, charitable and imaginative. You are susceptible to outside influences and need peace and seclusion from time to time.

PLUTO

You suppress a part of yourself that would love greater control. Strange behavior results from this and reveals subtly how you feel. Are you really so bad, to hold yourself back like this?

ARIES

Aries is the first constellation of the modern western zodiac and is symbolized by the Ram.

FAVORABLE TRAITS pioneering, enterprising, adventurous, brave, direct, enthusiastic, active, autonomous
CHALLENGING TRAITS impatient, impulsive, rash, aggressive, egotistical, inconsiderate, selfish, temperamental

YOUR PLANETS IN ARIES

SUN

The creative power of the Sun burns brightly in Aries, so you're a strong character with plenty of get up and go. You are positive, enthusiastic and straightforward, living up to your direct approach.

MOON

You have passionate, fiery feelings that you express readily. You lose your temper spectacularly, but you forgive quickly and don't hold a grudge, although others find it harder to recover.

MERCURY

You are a decisive thinker and are suited to snap decisions on the spur of the moment. You find sustained attention and focus more difficult, so can be rushed and impatient in your approach.

VENUS

You are naïve and romantic, falling in love on impulse and for love alone. You wear your heart on your sleeve and are easily manipulated by those whose intentions are less easy to perceive.

MARS

You have enormous energy for ambitious projects that take up a lot of effort in the shorter term. Over the long haul you aren't so good. You'd rather move on to more exciting things.

JUPITER

You could spend time trying to fit in with others and become very angry as a consequence. You develop most by being yourself, by setting a unique example and by showing others the way.

SATURN

It can seem a battle doing what you want, in view of your responsibilities and of others' expectations. You should be careful not to grow hardened and embittered, or careless of human values.

URANUS

Uranus moves slowly with an impact that is largely generational. Those born with Uranus in Aries find revolutionary times where the responsibilities of the individual are concerned. The concept of personal freedom is accentuated.

NEPTUNE

Neptune has a generational impact. Its last transit of Aries was in 1875 and the next begins in 2025. It will call into question the concept of selfhood, fostering compassion and spirituality in our lives.

PLUTO

The impact of Pluto is protracted. It will make clear to a generation the importance of moderation. Pluto was last in Aries in 1853 and will return in 2066.

TAURUS

Taurus is the second constellation of the modern western zodiac and is symbolized by the Bull.

FAVORABLE TRAITS practical, patient, reliable, persistent, dependable, affectionate, cautious, determined
CHALLENGING TRAITS possessive, lazy, inflexible, stubborn, resentful, boring, self-indulgent, greedy

YOUR PLANETS IN TAURUS

SUN
You are steady, stable, dependable and determined. You are affectionate and need to feel comfortable—with nice clothes, good food and a cozy home. You love your routines and plan well in advance.

MOON
This is a strong placing. Your feelings can be slow to rouse, but remain for the long term once awoken. You are loyal, affectionate and kind. You make a faithful partner and a dependable friend.

MERCURY
You won't be rushed into making up your mind. You like to think through your options carefully, only reaching a decision after lengthy reflection. You are deliberate, risk-averse and very obstinate.

VENUS
Love is one thing, your security and material safety are quite another. Much as you are affectionate, when it comes to more serious involvements you aren't about to take a risk.

MARS
Instantaneous action is not a concept you embrace. You need time to think and to prepare, plus time to wind up and then down again. What's the hurry in any case?

JUPITER
It is vital to develop your ideas on what is really important and to quantify this within your value system. A purely materialistic viewpoint can attract, but is no substitute for inner satisfaction.

SATURN
You are inclined to work on building your security as a buttress against potential hard times. An early upset could precipitate this preoccupation, which is only unhelpful if carried to extremes.

URANUS
Uranus is primarily a generational influence and spends around seven years in each sign. It was last in Taurus in 1942, showing a time during which the basic security of many was extensively disrupted.

NEPTUNE
Neptune's influence is generational, causing the just and compassionate distribution of material resources to become an important philosophical, religious and moral issue. Neptune was last here in 1889 and will not return until 2038.

PLUTO
The passage of Pluto through Taurus takes over 30 years and marks a period during which values globally will be turned on their head. Pluto left Taurus in 1884 and won't return until 2095.

GEMINI

Gemini is the third constellation of the modern western zodiac and is symbolized by the Heavenly Twins.

FAVORABLE TRAITS versatile, adaptable, lively, intelligent, communicative, busy, spontaneous, witty
CHALLENGING TRAITS anxious, nervous, superficial, unsettled, cunning, irresolute, scattered, inconsistent

YOUR PLANETS IN GEMINI

SUN

You are quite a butterfly and like to keep moving around. You are sociable and active and need plenty of intellectual stimulation to stop you from getting bored. You don't like doing anything for too long.

MOON

One day you feel one way and then another way on the next. Your passions are not deep and your feelings are prone to fluctuation. You like to analyze your emotions in rational terms.

MERCURY

You are bright, witty, clever and good with words, but your boredom threshold is extremely low. You need to keep your mind and body active for best results, or nervousness and anxiety can result.

VENUS

Nobody will ever possess you physically without initially capturing your mind. You are drawn to those who can charm you with their words. You prefer an impressive vocabulary to a bulging anatomy any day!

MARS

You are driven to communicate, either verbally, in writing or in other more individual ways. Discord is a consequence of not using these talents fully. You are forceful in expression and passionate in debate.

JUPITER

It is disadvantageous to spread yourself too thinly. You are curious and try to learn something about everything you can. You are adaptable and ingenious, although a deeper knowledge is sometimes to be preferred.

SATURN

You could underestimate the force of your imagination, the strength of your insight and the power of positive thought. You may try to limit your thinking to those topics with a strictly practical application.

URANUS

This placing favors inventions, new ideas and new schools of thought. Last occurring during the 1940s, it coincided with many innovative technological developments. Many others have subsequently been devised by those born around this time.

NEPTUNE

Neptune left Gemini in 1901, not to return until 2051. Its presence will enhance the artistic and musical heritage of the world at large. A resurgence in religious and spiritual thinking can be expected.

PLUTO

Pluto left Gemini in 1914, after 32 years transforming world transportation, along with global thinking as a result. It will not return this century.

CANCER

Cancer is the fourth constellation of the modern western zodiac and is symbolized by the Crab.

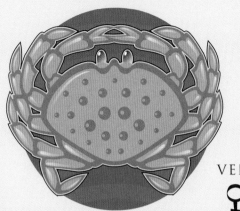

FAVORABLE TRAITS protective, nurturing, parental, kind, sympathetic, tenacious, thrifty, shrewd
CHALLENGING TRAITS hypersensitive, overemotional, unforgiving, crabby, cowardly, moody, touchy, snappy

YOUR PLANETS IN CANCER

SUN

Your home life is important and the relationship with your mother is a strong one. It may not always be harmonious but will exert a powerful influence, both during your childhood and far beyond.

MOON

Despite other influences that may sometimes persuade you to the contrary, you will never feel truly happy and fulfilled without a home of your own and the love of a family to surround you.

MERCURY

The ideas that enveloped you during childhood, the views of your parents and of your mother in particular, have been an enormous influence. This can make you timid and afraid to try new things.

VENUS

Marriage and a family can bring much joy. Ideally you love your current home and have happy memories of your childhood circumstances. Wherever you go you seek places that remind you of home.

MARS

How you feel has a big impact on your energy levels. You are full of zest when you are happy and secure, but when sad and dejected you are irritable and much more lethargic.

JUPITER

Growth comes for you through nurturing and caring and by allowing others to nurture and to care for you. Such an atmosphere is best fostered throughout life within an encouraging and supportive home environment.

SATURN

Emotional security begins at home. You need it so much that you act as if you don't as a camouflage. An impenetrable exterior is fine, but unless you're careful, loneliness and isolation can result.

URANUS

Uranus was last in Cancer between 1949 and 1956. Those born then have since been instrumental in a complete overhaul of domestic customs, traditions and social expectations. Uranus will not return to this sign until 2032.

NEPTUNE

Neptune is exalted in Cancer, an especially helpful placing. This is because as the old adage goes, charity begins at home. Neptune left this sign in 1916 and returns in 2065.

PLUTO

This generation lived through two world wars and saw death and destruction on a scale never before witnessed. Much was in the name of national allegiance, a concept approaching that of family.

LEO

Leo is the fifth constellation of the modern western zodiac and is symbolized by the Lion.

FAVORABLE TRAITS magnanimous, generous, noble, chivalrous, creative, expansive, dramatic, wholehearted
CHALLENGING TRAITS pompous, snobbish, conceited, spoiled, obstinate, bombastic, affected, a show-off

YOUR PLANETS IN LEO

SUN

The Sun placed here enhances solar traits. Many born under this influence are extrovert in consequence. You might seem quieter than expected, but will still command attention with your demeanor.

MOON

You have a real need to be noticed and appreciated. Without some kind of recognition you lose interest in what you are doing. You can work hard, but think play is much more fun.

MERCURY

You are stubborn and take ages forming opinions or subsequently changing them. It is good to be sure of your views, just as others deserve the same respect when they are sure of theirs.

VENUS

You seek godlike perfection in a lover, so even those who can rise to the initial challenge will be unlikely to do so forever. Unless you are careful, serial monogamy becomes the norm.

MARS

You are turned on by success. You seek to take action on a heroic scale. You have a talent for leadership, a proud and fiery spirit and a loathing of the mundane.

JUPITER

You are attracted to pomp, grandeur and ceremony and would like everything you do to be imposing and impressive. You will grow most by being yourself and by cultivating your creative instincts.

SATURN

You're reserved and hold yourself aloof from other people, especially in a group situation. A dignified personal bearing is a wonderful thing, but are you sure you don't just think it is all beneath you?

URANUS

Uranus was in Leo between 1955 and 1962, when the phenomenon of the teenager first became widely noted, marking a great step forward in the quest for personal differentiation. Uranus returns here in 2039.

NEPTUNE

Neptune passed through Leo from 1914 to 1929. This period was characterized by much idealism, but also by confusion in human relationships and by the emergence of significant new thinking in both music and art.

PLUTO

Pluto left Leo in 1958, having entered in 1937. The difference in average personal expectations between these two dates is substantial, with many much more able to exert a creative impact for themselves.

VIRGO

Virgo is the sixth constellation of the modern western zodiac and is symbolized by the Maiden.

FAVORABLE TRAITS analytical, modest, helpful, conscientious, meticulous, painstaking, diligent, tidy
CHALLENGING TRAITS overanalytical, uneasy, critical, tense, fussy, picky, inhibited, a wallflower

YOUR PLANETS IN VIRGO

SUN

You excel at the kind of difficult and detailed work that other people find impossible. You have a reputation for being critical, although actually you are hardest on yourself.

MOON

You are always analyzing your feelings and dissecting your emotions. This makes you rational in a crisis, but less good at understanding, for example, the beauty of love.

MERCURY

You are adept at the acquisition of specialist skills and methodologies, which may find application in your work. You are concerned with your health and with promoting correct dietary practices.

VENUS

A potential partner must meet high standards. They should be happy, healthy, hard-working, clean, practical, articulate—and more. Without abandoning your idealism, how do you feel about staying single?

MARS

Useful work is a way of life and something that you really respect. You have the energy and vitality if you take care. You could pursue a link with handicrafts or with the skilled use of tools.

JUPITER

You are naturally responsible and put duty before pleasure, so don't have any problems when prioritizing your obligations. It can be harder to relax, though, so make a special effort to have some fun.

SATURN

Saturn and Virgo together mean discipline, perfectionism, and adherence to the work ethic. This is marvelous in moderation, but in excess causes worry, inhibition, anxiety and health issues.

URANUS

The last Uranus in Virgo generation was born during the 1960s and has seen both working practices and health procedures revolutionized. In the main, jobs for life no longer exist and alternative therapies flourish.

NEPTUNE

Neptune was in Virgo between 1928 and 1943. Some born then believe the chance to dream is simply idle fantasy, as practical considerations clip the wings on which your imagination might soar.

PLUTO

During the transit of Pluto through Virgo that ended in 1972, it was also joined by Uranus, giving an even more transformative but ultimately regenerative slant on both your health affairs and working life.

LIBRA

Libra is the seventh constellation of the modern western zodiac and is symbolized by the Scales.

FAVORABLE TRAITS diplomatic, sociable, refined, harmonious, charming, agreeable, cultured, easygoing
CHALLENGING TRAITS indecisive, gullible, frivolous, changeable, weak, two-faced, argumentative, overcompromising

YOUR PLANETS IN LIBRA

SUN
You are plagued with indecision, so need other people to make up your mind. You can interact on either a cooperative or more competitive basis, although you are probably happier when everybody gets along.

MOON
This placing can be a blessing, or more of a trial. You need close partnerships, which is fine if you realize it, but not so good if you don't. Much depends on other influences.

MERCURY
I used to be indecisive, but now I'm not so sure. It's an old joke, but one that describes your thoughts perfectly, as you float happily along the path of least resistance.

VENUS
You have a penchant for luxury and could overspend. You may be creative or artistic, but love really makes your world go around. You can't imagine being single and would loathe every desperate moment.

MARS
On your own, you find it hard to get anything done. You take every opportunity to involve other people in whatever you are doing. Even a degree of friction helps to move things along.

JUPITER
You will develop most by looking at your closest relationships and especially any difficult issues that seem to have arisen over and over again. It is through others that you will learn about yourself.

SATURN
This is a strong placing for Saturn, since elements of caution, justice and loyalty are brought into the equation by this planet, whose harder edges are gently rounded by Libra's inherent finesse and tact.

URANUS
Last in Libra between 1968 and 1975, Uranus shows a generation that will seek to overturn traditional relationship concepts. Some might find this disruptive, others will welcome the fresh air.

NEPTUNE
You have witnessed the slow and gradual disintegration of relationship conventions and expectations. New concepts have arisen, initially motivated by idealism and then by the sober consequences of experience.

PLUTO
Should the impact of Uranus and Neptune during recent decades not have irrevocably altered your view of personal relationships, the life path of those with Pluto in Libra will ensure this is the case.

SCORPIO

Scorpio is the eighth constellation of the modern western zodiac and is symbolized by the Scorpion.

FAVORABLE TRAITS deep, intense, resolute, powerful, loyal, discerning, intuitive, subtle
CHALLENGING TRAITS jealous, vindictive, vengeful, secretive, suspicious, pitiless, twisted, malicious

YOUR PLANETS IN SCORPIO

SUN
You have a strong personality, some fixed ideas and an absorbing inner life. Much of what goes on below the surface is not apparent, since you strive to keep many things to yourself.

MOON
Emotions are intended to be felt and swiftly released. The ability to shut down your feelings is admirable in a crisis, but can easily lead to brooding and suppression in the longer term.

MERCURY
You are an excellent judge of character. You can strike just where it hurts. You have an awesome memory and file things away in your head. Most times, though, you say nothing at all.

VENUS
You love to the depths of your being. Leaping from cliffs into crocodile-infested waters would be nothing for the one you loved. Probably as a consequence, you are cautious of getting involved.

MARS
This placing is linked with sex, although you are similarly passionate about many things. Essentially, whatever you do, you commit wholeheartedly, or else you'd rather not bother.

JUPITER
The more you understand your own complexity, trying to explain your inner thoughts and to appreciate the sensitivities of others, the more happiness and fulfillment will be yours.

SATURN
You have immense self-control, but also many profound changes to go through. From time to time you must relax your iron grip, since a healthy emotional maturity cannot be achieved otherwise.

URANUS
A strong placing, since both features share a link with change and transformation. Those born under this collective influence must establish a sense of perspective, since their combined manifestation can be extreme.

NEPTUNE
This generation has fashioned a resurgence in spiritual concerns. Many of those involved in the holistic movement were born between 1956 and 1970, during the period of this transit.

PLUTO
Pluto passed through Scorpio between 1983 and 1995. Those born then will instigate and witness much transformation, with the challenge to ensure that this happens only when necessary and solely with the highest motivations.

SAGITTARIUS

Sagittarius is the ninth constellation and is symbolized by the Archer.

FAVORABLE TRAITS cheerful, optimistic, tolerant, freedom-loving, adventurous, philosophical, honest, sincere
CHALLENGING TRAITS tactless, careless, blunt, clumsy, reckless, untidy, over-the-top, exaggerated

YOUR PLANETS IN SAGITTARIUS

SUN
You are jovial, boisterous, outgoing and exuberant, always ready for a good time and to try something new. You take huge risks and get away with them, while those around you gasp in amazement!

MOON
You are optimistic and happy-go-lucky, so don't let your troubles get you down. You are hurt when others fail to meet your expectations, but are often tolerant enough to forgive them anyway.

MERCURY
If you're not careful, you could end up promising more than you can deliver. The management of time and detail is not your strongest point, although you are much better at the broad overview.

VENUS
You regard your relationships as a voyage of discovery and are less concerned with your ultimate destination. If you feel there is nothing to look forward to, you might start growing bored and restive.

MARS
You need lots of open space and the freedom to let off steam. You don't like to feel restricted either physically or emotionally, and grow clumsy in small spaces as you try to move about.

JUPITER
You have your own set of philosophical and religious principles by which you will run your life. Your ideas are philanthropic, more radical in youth and increasingly mainstream with maturity.

SATURN
You are keen to develop your ideas, but could disregard those that don't reach your stringent criteria surrounding usefulness. It would be a shame to reject more adventurous concepts.

URANUS
Freedom of thought and belief will be a major issue for this generation, born between 1981 and 1988. In combination these influences can be radical, so fanaticism and extremism will need to be addressed.

NEPTUNE
Neptune was last in Sagittarius between 1970 and 1984. In many ways this is a continuation of Neptune through Scorpio, as newly emergent spiritual beliefs become gradually incorporated into mainstream schools of thought.

PLUTO
With a ponderously slow orbit, Pluto's transit of a sign often highlights the concerns of society. Between 1995 and 2008, these interests will include philosophy, nationality, immigration and religion.

CAPRICORN

Capricorn is the tenth constellation of the modern western zodiac and is symbolized by the Sea-Goat.

FAVORABLE TRAITS ambitious, assiduous, conservative, sensible, constant, self-disciplined, responsible, realistic
CHALLENGING TRAITS pessimistic, calculating, miserable, mean, inhibited, strict, stern, rigid

YOUR PLANETS IN CAPRICORN

SUN

You are ambitious, responsible and frugal and often emphasize your career. You like to be busy and have an old head on young shoulders from your earliest days. Generally then, life gets better with age.

MOON

Furthering your objectives makes you happy and fulfilled. You place practicalities first and prove yourself through ambition and accomplishment. Your emotional well-being is often far down on your list.

MERCURY

You have a good head for business and can usually spot an opportunity to advance your interests. You plan carefully and develop your strategy, but might be overly guarded and cautious in your approach.

VENUS

You are reserved when expressing your feelings and take a long time getting to know someone really well. You don't have lots of friends, but those you have you rely on and trust.

MARS

You like to take your time, to think things through and then to apply yourself over the longer term. You certainly appreciate the value of hard work.

JUPITER

This placing affects all those born during a 12-month period every 12 years. It can be good for your career concerns, as long as you don't neglect your personal life.

SATURN

You feel driven to work and attain a genuine satisfaction from so doing. Remember that ruthless and calculating attitudes are best confined to the business world. Emotional needs are very real ones too.

URANUS

Those born between 1988 and 1995 with Uranus in Capricorn are set to revitalize the social order. This period saw the collapse of institutions across the world that were long overdue for restructuring.

NEPTUNE

This transit began in 1984 and concluded in 1998. Even established governments had to demonstrate their awareness of more esoteric issues, involving compassion for the planet and for humanity at large.

PLUTO

Pluto next enters Capricorn in 2008 and stays for 16 years. Last in this position at the beginning of the Industrial Revolution, we can expect similar change and phenomenal progress this time around.

AQUARIUS

Aquarius is the eleventh constellation of the modern western zodiac and is symbolized by the Water-Bearer.

FAVORABLE TRAITS progressive, humanitarian, egalitarian, independent, unconventional, friendly, fair, rational
CHALLENGING TRAITS contrary, rebellious, eccentric, perverse, self-willed, erratic, unstable, cold

YOUR PLANETS IN AQUARIUS

SUN
You are an individualist with your own style. You care about the bigger issues, any number of causes and the future of mankind. You are great at friendship, but can find closer liaisons limiting.

MOON
You are extremely independent with an overwhelming need to go your own way. If you are in touch with your emotions then success is yours, otherwise you could end up sabotaging your best intentions.

MERCURY
You have a brilliant mind that combines the inspirational with the rational. You favor innovative ideas and progressive methodologies, you embrace new technologies and you communicate well.

VENUS
You love your independence and you love your friends, but closer than that and you soon start having difficulties. You'll get on best with people like you, who have their own interests too.

MARS
You are sociable and a team player, but you aren't afraid to go your own way and to have some unusual views. You are proud to be a little different.

JUPITER
Jupiter shows luck, success and personal development.
Aquarius shows uniqueness, individuality and the new. Together they bring good fortune, through the development of your independent interests and unusual ideas.

SATURN
Saturn placed in the sign most connected with society and with groups shows that whatever you feel you must achieve, it won't ultimately mean anything unless it has some relevance to other people too.

URANUS
Those born with Uranus in Aquarius are capable of manifesting Aquarian principles in their purest form. Often groundbreaking, it will be a matter of collective responsibility to ensure these remain tempered with moderation.

NEPTUNE
Neptune entered Aquarius in 1998 and will leave in 2012.
This marks a rare period for the development of scientific technique, one during which we will all get to understand the subtle mysteries of life much more completely.

PLUTO
Pluto enters Aquarius in 2023 and was last there during the final quarter of the 18th century. This was a peak time for technological development, and it would not be surprising to see that surpassed.

PISCES

Pisces is the final constellation of the modern western zodiac and is symbolized by the Fishes.

FAVORABLE TRAITS compassionate, caring, charitable, receptive, idealistic, psychic, imaginative, unassuming
CHALLENGING TRAITS impractical, vague, helpless, confused, unreliable, disorganized, manipulative, escapist

YOUR PLANETS IN PISCES

SUN

You are kind and helpful, humble and unassuming and you seek to avoid the spotlight. Although you seem easy-going, you soon develop a fine understanding of what is right for you.

MOON

You are a true and incurable romantic. You dream, over the domestic chores, of handsome knights on gallant steeds and fair maidens in need of rescuing. You are imaginative, creative and a sensitive soul.

MERCURY

You remember impressions and feelings much better than dates and times. You should try to express yourself creatively. Music is helpful in times of discouragement and stress.

VENUS

Many religions talk of the love that their leaders show for the world. This is the universal spiritual love of this placing, the love of charity workers and of those who sacrifice themselves.

MARS

Mars and Pisces don't go together well, since although this is an excellent placing for the selfless and compassionate assistance of others, it isn't so helpful when it comes to furthering your own concerns.

JUPITER

Jupiter and Pisces share an affinity, since the former ruled the latter before Neptune was discovered. Often this is a helpful placing, providing you don't always put others before yourself.

SATURN

Those born during a 30-month period all have this placing. Often its main impact is to make you worry, since defining clear boundaries can be difficult through a hazy, receptive Piscean lens.

URANUS

Uranus entered Pisces during 2003 and leaves during 2011. This placing is strengthened by Neptune's passage through Aquarius, presenting together an important opportunity to raise our value system on a global scale.

NEPTUNE

Neptune enters Pisces during 2011 and remains for 15 years. Last in this position during the middle of the 19th century, this period saw increased philanthropy in richer nations.

PLUTO

Pluto was last in Pisces during 1823 and won't return for some decades. We can expect Pluto to regenerate the fundamental basis of our belief systems and to encourage a more experiential approach.

THE TEN PLANETS

The planets reveal different components of your psychological makeup. Each of the planets represents a different part of your personality.

THE SUN—CHARACTER

As the central body of our solar system, the Sun enjoys a pivotal position within astrological interpretation. Sun-sign astrology is relatively straightforward and has served to stimulate the interest of many. The Sun shows your essential character, your sense of self, your ego and the characteristics you consciously express. Being yourself is a creative act and you are happy to display those traits linked with your Sun sign. You express them fully through the house involved.

FAVORABLE TRAITS creative, outgoing, confident, vibrant, dignified, charismatic, magnanimous, expressive **CHALLENGING TRAITS** arrogant, egotistical, condescending, overbearing, self-important, self-absorbed, gushing, inflated

THE MOON—EMOTIONS

The Moon also has special status and circuits the zodiac in one month. Whereas the Sun symbolizes your conscious side, the Moon highlights your more subconscious needs. It shows your feelings and emotions, your inner wants and motivations, persistent habits that have become ingrained and subliminal behavior patterns that are often instinctive, conditioned and inherited. On a very real level, the Moon shows what you need from life. It shows your underlying temperament and how you respond without thinking.

FAVORABLE TRAITS imaginative, sensitive, nurturing, sympathetic, kind, caring, receptive, shrewd **CHALLENGING TRAITS** moody, changeable, weak, gullible, snappy, illogical, irrational, unstable

MERCURY—THINKING AND COMMUNICATION

Mercury is the first of what astrologers call the personal planets, because it moves swiftly enough around the zodiac to make a difference on a personal and individual level. Mercury shows the logical and reasoned component of your intellect, your rational mind, what you think about and how you communicate, whether through speech, writing or more subtle means, like touch. It is indicative of your thought processes and your intellectual faculties, and is closely related to intelligence and learning.

FAVORABLE TRAITS curious, communicative, intelligent, perceptive, versatile, articulate, rational, analytical
CHALLENGING TRAITS inconsistent, devious, nervous, argumentative, sarcastic, unfeeling, cunning, neurotic

VENUS—LOVE AND AFFECTION

Venus is a personal planet and is never more than two signs from the Sun. Venus is the planet of love and reveals much about your attitude toward relationships. It shows what appeals to your affections and the ways you express your own love. To some degree Venus also shows your personal values and aesthetic sensibilities, through its links with money, comfort, possessions and pleasure.

FAVORABLE TRAITS harmonious, tactful, gracious, diplomatic, refined, attractive, sociable, tasteful
CHALLENGING TRAITS lazy, indecisive, impractical, silly, dependent, superficial, non-confrontational, a doormat

MARS—ENERGY AND DESIRE

Mars is the final personal planet and circuits the zodiac in under two years. It is connected with activity, initiative, strength, motivation and drive. It shows your physical energy levels, your basic wants and desires, your libido, the impulse to prove yourself and your competitive instincts. Mars shows the areas of life where conflict can be expected and why this is likely to occur. It describes the qualities you find sexually attractive and your own approach to physical intimacy.

FAVORABLE TRAITS decisive, assertive, active, energetic, brave, positive, pioneering, direct
CHALLENGING TRAITS aggressive, angry, brutal, foolish, selfish, violent, rude, coarse

SATURN—STRUCTURE

Saturn is the second social planet and is in the same sign for everyone born within an approximate 30-month period, although the house placing and any aspects will vary. Saturn serves to redefine the areas in which we most need structure and organization, but does this by bringing with it problems, frustrations and arduous responsibilities along the way. Saturn is connected with the super-ego and with the impact of paternal influences. A sense of wisdom, patience and maturity eventually evolves.

FAVORABLE TRAITS ambitious, responsible, patient, practical, cautious, sensible, disciplined, realistic
CHALLENGING TRAITS severe, acquisitive, miserable, cruel, dogmatic, strict, repressed, cold

JUPITER—ABUNDANCE

Jupiter is the first of the so-called social planets, remaining in each sign for one year and affecting all those born during this time. It represents growth, expansion, abundance, success and good luck. Jupiter shows where you will enjoy good fortune and the ways you can best broaden your experience, develop your personal understanding and enhance your material success. The main downside of this planet can be a considerable temptation to go overboard!

FAVORABLE TRAITS optimistic, generous, jovial, benevolent, tolerant, philosophical, broad-minded, wise
CHALLENGING TRAITS overindulgent, over-optimistic, wasteful, unreliable, rash, insensitive, slapdash, bombastic

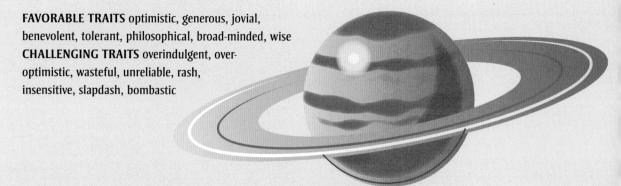

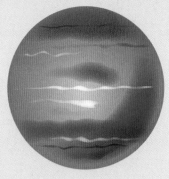

URANUS— INDIVIDUALITY AND CHANGE

Uranus is the closest of the three outer planets and was discovered in 1781. It is assessed according to its house position and with regard to any aspects. Uranus shows the unusual and the new, independence, originality and surprise. It embodies the twin attributes of freedom and individuality and regularly heralds the unexpected, together with a preference for self-determination and for liberty. Uranus also affects your choice of friends and the groups with which you are involved.

FAVORABLE TRAITS independent, surprising, original, inventive, progressive, objective, detached, impartial
CHALLENGING TRAITS awkward, difficult, eccentric, rebellious, obstinate, aloof, misfit, extreme

NEPTUNE— DREAMS AND INTUITION

Neptune is the second of the outer planets. It governs everything that is misty, intangible, amorphous, mysterious and hard to define—even this planet's discovery in 1846 was shrouded in controversy. Neptune confers faith, idealism, spirituality, self-sacrifice, intuition and creativity, although overidealism, self-deception and delusion are constant possibilities. Essentially Neptune shows where you are at your most sensitive, imaginative and idealistic, but also where you are most prone to ending up disappointed, disillusioned, hurt and let down.

FAVORABLE TRAITS idealistic, intuitive, imaginative, mystical, compassionate, subtle, inspired, psychic
CHALLENGING TRAITS devious, deceptive, impractical, gullible, clouded, escapist, manipulative, a martyr

PLUTO—DEPTH, POWER AND TRANSFORMATION

Pluto is currently the outermost planet in our solar system, confirmed for the first time in 1930. It is linked with transformation and regeneration, with a powerful force and with inexorable change. Pluto shows your ability to address your conditioning and to transform negative influences into something more constructive. Its effects are subtle, gradual, momentous and complete. Pluto shows where it is likely that this energy will become a significant focus, as well as where you will always want to be in control.

FAVORABLE TRAITS regenerative, transformative, determined, persistent, dedicated, deep, loyal, intense
CHALLENGING TRAITS jealous, possessive, bitter, twisted, controlling, obsessive, sadistic, destructive

INTERPRETATION ESSENTIALS

THE ANGLES

The angles are important components of any birth chart. Really they function as two interconnected axes, rather than as four separate points.

UNDERSTANDING THE ANGLES

ASCENDANT (asc) Relates specifically to your outer personality and to the image you present.

DESCENDANT (dsc) Pertains to your closest relationships, especially those on an intimate one-to-one basis.

MIDHEAVEN (mc) Shows your perfect image of yourself. Connected also with your ambitions and career.

IMUM COELI (ic) Further information on your emotional needs, upbringing and your home life.

THE ASC/DSC THROUGH THE SIGNS

ARIES/LIBRA
You are positive and dynamic, even when feeling completely the opposite. You need other people, because otherwise how will you always come first?

TAURUS/SCORPIO
You give the impression of being comfortable. Often you are well turned-out. You seem very stable and placid, but are jealous and possessive in your closest relationships.

GEMINI/SAGITTARIUS
You don't appreciate people trying to cramp your style. You need lots of variety and intellectual stimulation in your day. You hate sitting still and are easily bored.

CANCER/CAPRICORN
You seem sensitive and nurturing and are completely dependable in your closest relationships. You get involved slowly, but are very committed.

LEO/AQUARIUS
You are dignified and charismatic and your persona is somehow striking. Unfortunately you tend to attract the wrong partners, since they are far too rebellious, unpredictable and independent.

VIRGO/PISCES
You let others command the spotlight and seem modest, retiring and shy. You are idealistic in relationships and like to be helpful to those you love.

LIBRA/ARIES
On the face of it, you present a sociable and diplomatic demeanor. You appreciate the importance of harmonious interpersonal interaction.

SCORPIO/TAURUS
You are rather intense and very possessive over those you love. You try not to give your feelings away, but your inner machinations are obvious to many.

SAGITTARIUS/GEMINI
You feel a positive outlook is a good thing. You don't like restrictions and have a special affinity with the countryside and with wide-open spaces.

CAPRICORN/CANCER
You always try to say and do the right thing. You have a strong sense of propriety and an innate sensitivity to the needs and expectations of others.

♒ ♌ AQUARIUS/LEO
When you give your heart, you really mean it. You are proud and staunchly loyal in close relationships. You aren't too showy, but are certainly a little different.

♓ ♍ PISCES/VIRGO
You are extremely idealistic and can go through life like a poor lost soul. When it comes to your closest associations, you are more discriminating than you appear.

THE MC/IC THROUGH THE SIGNS

♈ ♎ ARIES/LIBRA
You feel best able to pursue your objectives and your career aspirations once you are certain of a harmonious partnership and of a peaceful environment within your home.

♉ ♏ TAURUS/SCORPIO
You feel best suited to a solid and traditional position within the community. What happens at home is far more personal, though. Your privacy is zealously maintained.

♊ ♐ GEMINI/SAGITTARIUS
There are so many intriguing possibilities, if only you could decide. Nonetheless, one thing is for sure. You don't want anybody telling you what time to be home.

♋ ♑ CANCER/CAPRICORN
You need to feel nurtured and accepted. You want to find somewhere that you really belong. Once happy within yourself, you provide safety and security for others too.

♌ ♒ LEO/AQUARIUS
You are a star, a unique individual, and you want to shine. You could never be happy with mediocrity and so endeavor to stand out from the rest.

♍ ♓ VIRGO/PISCES
Your approach is practical, hard-working and persevering. Underneath it all you are sensitive and idealistic, so may not want to aim too high for fear of disappointment.

♎ ♈ LIBRA/ARIES
You have a lot of latent energy that needs guidance. You should aim for a peaceful and balanced outlook, ideally with a partnership component.

♏ ♉ SCORPIO/TAURUS
Home is a haven of comfort and security for you. You are certain of your objectives and pursue these vigorously, yet your overall direction still changes several times.

♐ ♊ SAGITTARIUS/GEMINI
Your horizons are expansive and your possibilities almost endless. Sitting around at home is not recommended, unless there is something interesting to do, learn or talk about.

♑ ♋ CAPRICORN/CANCER
Your main aims and your career aspirations are both quite traditional. Your outlook is orthodox and favors the long view. Your home life assumes a conventional tone.

♒ ♌ AQUARIUS/LEO
You want to be a part of things, but like to feel different too. You thrive on individual attention, but don't want others to feel neglected.

♓ ♍ PISCES/VIRGO
It would help to clarify what your security might ideally comprise. Life is a sea of infinite potential, so personal ambition could seem an unworthy choice.

THE MAJOR ASPECTS—FINE TUNING

From an interpretative perspective, aspects can be considered in two ways. First, they show the components of your birth chart that are working well together and those features that are likely to cause more discord. Second, when two planets, or a planet and another birth chart feature, are in aspect to one another, the influence of both is modified and changed, either subtly or much more so.

Hard aspects are inherently stressful and soft aspects are those that naturally function well. It is important, though, to remember that we develop the most through our hard aspects. In turning a less favorable expression around to a positive, there is often more potential than that augured by a beneficial combination in the first place.

There are hundreds of possible aspects between the main chart features, so it is hard to remember a detailed delineation for each one. Add to this the extensive number of house and sign combinations and it soon becomes essential to have some way of working matters out yourself.

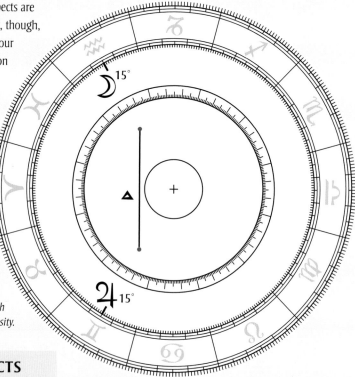

Moon in Aquarius trine Jupiter in Gemini shows that your independent and individualistic emotional nature is inherently in harmony with your enquiring mind and endless curiosity.

UNDERSTANDING THE ASPECTS

aspect	hard or soft?	key words
conjunction	hard	combines with
sextile	soft	works with
square	hard	conflicts with
trine	soft	works perfectly with
opposition	hard	opposes

A useful technique involves aspect key words, in combination with the planetary key words from earlier in this chapter. For example:
- Sun sextile Moon—your conscious self and your emotions work well together.
- Sun square Moon—your conscious self and your emotions conflict.

METHOD ONE

The first method of considering your aspects means thinking about the symbolism of the partners in the aspectual equation. Why might there be a harmonious or more stressful flow of energy between them? For example, consider this birth chart, where the Moon in the Second House squares Jupiter in the Fifth. This means that your emotional need for security is challenged by the love you have of taking risks. This would be a very different effect from Moon in the Tenth House square Jupiter in the Seventh, where the expansive nature of your relationships is distracting you from your career.

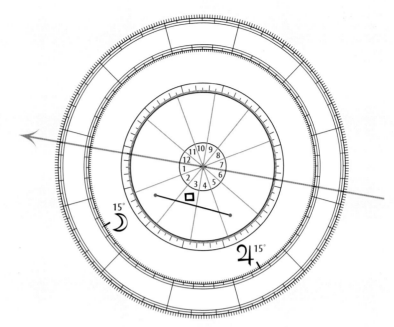

Moon in the Second House square Jupiter in the Fifth causes problems when your basic security becomes threatened by your penchant for wild risks.

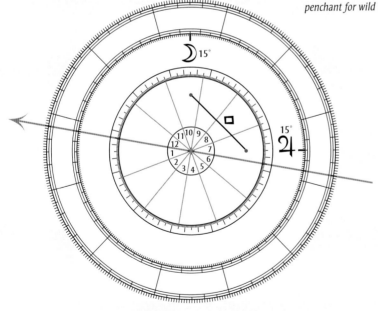

Moon in the Tenth House square Jupiter in the Seventh causes upset when your closest associations are in conflict with your personal goals.

Moon square Jupiter is an aspect of emotional excess. This downside of Jupiter is accentuated by the stressful nature of the square, thus impacting unfavorably on your feelings as symbolized by the Moon. Fortunately, Jupiter has blessed you with abundant emotions that you are able to express constructively, but the hard aspect ensures you should always take care, as you work consciously or unconsciously toward a more lasting equilibrium. This ongoing process is known by astrologers as personal development, or often more simply as growth.

Soft aspects flow together and tend to work in the background without us being consciously aware. Sextiles take some effort, but trines are simply "how we are."

METHOD TWO

When aspects are made to the luminaries and the personal planets, it is recommended that you take your aspect analysis a stage further. Pick a key word for each feature (see box, right). Always refer to your planets in the order they are listed in your aspects table, Sun through to Pluto and then on until the Moon's Node. This is known as the correct *planetary protocol*.

The planet that comes first in the equation is being aspected, the second one is doing the aspecting. The facet of personality shown by the aspected planet, so long as it is a personal planet or a luminary, will be affected either in a favorable or less favorable way by the aspecting planet, depending on whether a hard or a soft aspect is involved.

For example, Venus in hard aspect to Uranus could mean the more challenging facets of Uranus are all too obvious in your love life. You suffer a series of broken relationships and attract partners who are less than reliable.

By contrast Venus in soft aspect to Uranus confers favorable Uranus characteristics. You like unusual people and prefer feeling free in your closest associations. With awareness you can still select this path if you have a harder aspect, but this takes effort first and constant action in the second place. Again, the emphasis on personal growth is accentuated.

KEY WORDS FOR THE PLANETS

Planet	Key words
Sun	your character
Moon	your emotions
Mercury	thinking and communication
Venus	love and affection
Mars	energy and desire
Jupiter	abundance
Saturn	structure
Uranus	individuality and change
Neptune	dreams and intuition
Pluto	depth, power and transformation

PLANETARY PROTOCOL

Planets	☉	☽	☿	♀	♂	♃	♄	♅	♆	♇	Asc	MC	NN
Sun	☉												
Moon		☽											
Mercury			☿										
Venus				♀									
Mars					♂								
Jupiter						♃							
Saturn							♄						
Uranus								♅					
Neptune									♆				
Pluto										♇			
Asc	Ruling planet												
MC	Rulers house										Asc	MC	N Node
N Node	Rising planet												

Aspects

FOR EXAMPLE

Here is an example involving two planetary pairs, with their combined expression slightly exaggerated in the interests of clarity. You'll see that favorable or more challenging traits are being expressed in each instance, depending on the aspect combination involved. (For a full list of favorable and challenging traits, see the characteristics listed under each planet on pages 84–87.)

Of the hard aspects, conjunctions have a mixed constructive and less constructive expression. Squares show an internal battle, oppositions are perceived as external and usually as the fault of others. However, all hard aspects can be raised through effort and growth to the same expression as a trine or sextile. The results of doing so are at least equivalent to their softer counterparts, but you will always need to ensure that a constructive expression is maintained.

All aspects to the Sun affect your character and conscious self, those to Mercury affect how you think and communicate. The aspectual traits linked with Mars and Saturn can be found in the planets section.

MARS ASPECTING A PLANET

Favorable traits for soft aspects	Challenging traits for hard aspects
energetic	rash
brave	aggressive
decisive	confrontational
leadership	violent
enthusiasm	rude

SATURN ASPECTING A PLANET

Favorable traits for soft aspects	Challenging traits for hard aspects
ambitious	miserable
responsible	dogmatic
patient	strict
practical	inhibited
sensible	cold
reliable	pessimistic

SUN/MARS

Conjunct (hard aspect)
You should keep on the go, otherwise you may grow restive and bad-tempered.

Sextile (soft aspect)
You are lively and active. You know you have more energy than most.

Square (hard aspect)
You are self-assertive and challenging. You don't shrink from provoking conflict.

Trine (soft aspect)
You are brave and have masses of energy. People wonder at all you do.

Opposition (hard aspect)
Life is full of conflict. You wonder why other people are so difficult.

MERCURY/SATURN

Conjunct (hard aspect)
You're a realist, although you tend toward the pessimistic.

Sextile (soft aspect)
You are cautious, patient and methodical. You are not given to fancy.

Square (hard aspect)
You look on the dark side. Not that you tell anyone, except to complain.

Trine (soft aspect)
You excel at details and planning. You never promise anything you can't deliver.

Opposition (hard aspect)
You feel put upon. Somehow people always mess up your plans.

FIRST IMPRESSIONS

CHART SHAPE

As you begin your investigations, you might expect every birth chart to have the ten planets spread about evenly, with no substantial groupings, emphasized areas, gaps or empty spaces. In practice, you'll find this is rarely the case. Charts are often characterized by clusters, clumps and groupings of planets that can occur anywhere.

Analyzing the shape of a birth chart and any planets highlighted is a great starting point for your interpretation. Although the balanced nature of a splash formation is often cited as ideal, in the horoscopes of those who reach public attention it remains an infrequent formation to encounter. It would seem that a less balanced state of affairs is a good indication of the drive and focus necessary, whenever the achievement of public fame or notoriety is concerned.

Remember that finding one of the more clearly defined formations in your own or any other horoscope cannot necessarily be seen as anything other than beneficial.

The analysis of chart shapes was defined by Marc Edmund Jones in the first part of the 20th century and has since been augmented and developed by astrologers worldwide. It remains based around the ten planets, so don't be tempted to bring Chiron or the Moon's node into the picture.

BUNDLE

This is the most concentrated formation and can occur anywhere in the chart. All the planets are contained within one third of the birth chart, 120 degrees or the space of four signs. The bundle formation helps mainly with focus and with concentration, but can seem less beneficial when other things start suffering as a consequence. Some leeway should be allowed when measuring this or any other shape, so if your chart has planets slightly outside the permissible range, you can still use your discretion when deciding which shape applies.

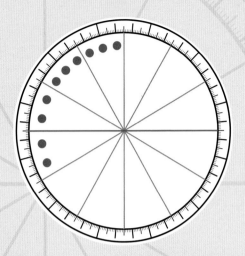

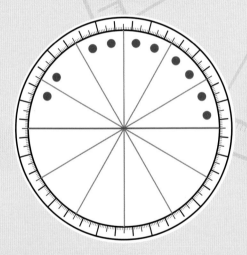

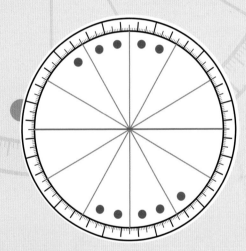

BOWL

Spreading out from the bundle in a bowl formation the planets occupy about half the birth chart, 180 degrees or the equivalent of six zodiac signs. Again some leeway is allowed, but a classic bowl chart has an opposition as the rim. Bowls can be found anywhere, to the left or the right of the chart, upside down in the uppermost hemisphere or the right way up at the bottom. As with the bundle, the bowl shows focus and places emphasis on the occupied houses and signs. There is now more awareness, though, of those areas that otherwise you might have been tempted to neglect.

SEESAW

As the name suggests, the seesaw configuration has two similar groupings of planets in approximate opposition. Each is contained within three signs or so and separated by unoccupied balancing spaces of sixty degrees or more. It is not surprising that those born under this configuration seem to have two very different sides, although such ambiguity can be useful when it comes to developing an objective viewpoint.

SLING

Otherwise known as the fan, this formation is based around the bundle, but has all the planets except one in the span of four signs. The isolated planet is known as the handle and must be at least sixty degrees distant from any other planet. Understanding this handle is the key from an interpretative perspective, since the isolated planet will need special attention to be brought into line with the rest. A lone planetary conjunction sometimes works in the same way.

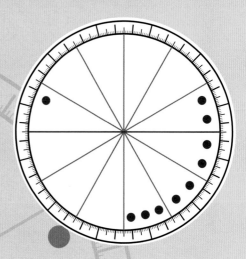

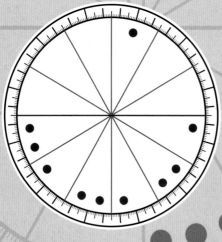

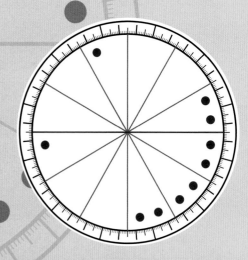

BUCKET

The same comments apply to both the sling and the bucket formation, except in the latter it is a bowl chart that is extended by the presence of an isolated planet. The same criteria and interpretative scenarios apply, with cases to be made for both a lessened and more pronounced need for integration.

WHEELBARROW

This shape is a recent addition, occurring when a bundle or bowl formation is balanced by two distinct but separate handles to give an overall impression reminiscent of the name. It is rare that the handles are both exactly the same distance away from the main body of this pattern, and your natural tendency will be to identify with the closest combination, while neglecting the potential of the furthest planetary pair.

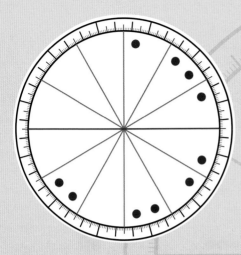

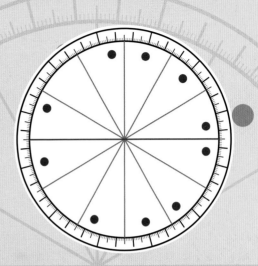

LOCOMOTIVE

Planets occupy two thirds of the birth chart, evenly spaced throughout an area of about eight signs. A space equivalent to four signs, or 120 degrees, is left empty. The engine of the locomotive formation is the first planet to move into this unoccupied area, according to the normal counterclockwise motion of the planets and disregarding any retrograde motion. In your diagram, it is the one in the Ninth House. The lives of locomotive people follow the symbolism of their lead planet, assessed according to the planet concerned, its house position, sign placing and any aspects made.

SPLASH

Probably what many would think of as a typical birth chart, the splash has an even distribution of planets. Every quadrant is occupied and there are no empty spaces of more than ninety degrees. Although from a developmental perspective such a broad spectrum of talent is enormously useful, it can be harder for splash people to focus or to concentrate their attention for long.

SPLAY

Similar to the splash in that planetary distribution is largely even, the splay is differentiated by at least one distinct grouping and the added interpretive focus such an emphasis implies. Since every splay chart is different, individuality is notable in all those born with this shape. Sometimes the planets form a tripod arrangement, conferring both an essential stability and widespread capabilities. If you cannot classify a birth chart in any other way, then it is probably a splay.

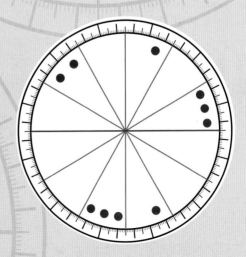

PLANETARY DISTRIBUTION

Once you have established the shape of your chart, you should next decide on the importance of the ways in which the planets are positioned around it.

Each shape of chart can fall anywhere, with the interpretation of a chart focused in the upper hemisphere being very different from that based mainly in the first six houses. There are two ways in which planetary distribution can be assessed. The first divides the chart into four quadrants, the second into two pairs of hemispheres. Clusters and groups of planets called stellia should also be noted, since these will emphasize the house and sign they occupy.

QUADRANT DIVISION

Quadrant division divides the birth chart into four, using the ascendant/descendant axis as one division and the cusps of the Fourth and Tenth Houses as the other. An alternative method uses the MC/IC axis as the second division, but an awkward disparity of quadrant size will often result.

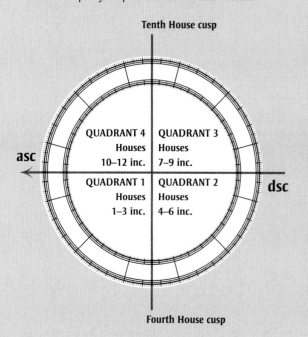

Tenth House cusp

asc

QUADRANT 4
Houses
10–12 inc.

QUADRANT 3
Houses
7–9 inc.

QUADRANT 1
Houses
1–3 inc.

QUADRANT 2
Houses
4–6 inc.

dsc

Fourth House cusp

To work with quadrant division, simply count how many planets are found in each one. Restrict your investigations to the ten planets and note in particular which quadrant, if any, appears the most crowded. More can be learned from other quadrants that might seem sparsely represented.

A balanced distribution could suggest a balanced nature, but this is a generality. Sometimes even a cursory investigation contradicts this, so do take care!

FIRST QUADRANT

With the majority of planets in the first quadrant, there is a strong focus on self. Although other placings will modify this, there is always the need for balance.

SECOND QUADRANT

An emphasis on the second quadrant shows a strong focus on home, children, work, health and everyday responsibilities. This quadrant is linked with creativity, fun and with making our lives what we want them to be. It emphasizes the affairs of the houses that are highlighted.

THIRD QUADRANT

The expansion of personal horizons is an underlying theme for those with a third quadrant dominance. Relationships, shared resources, a deeper perspective, travel and the development of your own beliefs and philosophy will all be instrumental in this process.

FOURTH QUADRANT

The fourth quadrant is linked with spiritual concerns, higher values, self-sacrifice, intuition and withdrawal. It is associated with groups and with humanitarian interests, with your contribution to society and with what you can achieve.

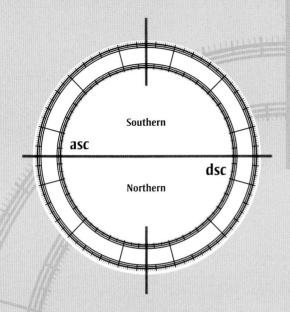

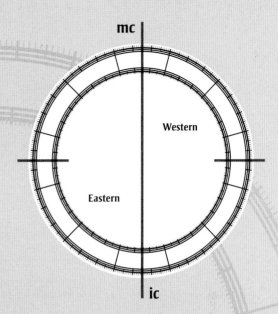

HEMISPHERE DIVISION

There are two ways in which the birth chart can be divided into hemispheres—horizontally along the ascendant/descendant axis, and vertically along an imaginary line connecting the MC/IC.

As a consequence of established traditions, the hemispheres of the birth chart are reversed, with the eastern to the left and the western to the right. The planets are visible when in the southern hemisphere at the top of your birth chart, and are out of view when below the horizon and in the northern hemisphere. The planets rise in the east—the ascendant side—and set in the west—the descendant side. It's a confusing scenario, but one that will sink in with time!

To take a look at hemisphere division, first divide your birth chart along the axis concerned and then simply count the planets on either side. Limit yourself to the ten planets only and do not count any other chart features. Few conclusions can be drawn from a 5/5 or even a 6/4 spread, with comments regarding a balanced nature not to be overstated at this early stage. A dominance of 7/3 or greater in either direction is certainly worthy of note.

NORTH/SOUTH

So much as you can describe anybody in one word, when the majority of planets are found in the southern hemisphere you are predominately an extrovert. You look for solutions outside of yourself when trouble threatens in your life. You are outgoing and try to make the most of your opportunities. When the majority of planets are in the northern hemisphere, you are much more shy and retiring. You are best described as an introvert, you are introspective and you have an active and absorbing inner life. Unsurprisingly, in times of trouble you look within yourself for strength and for solutions.

EAST/WEST

When most of your planets are in the eastern hemisphere, you are largely self-oriented and decide things mainly on the basis of your own requirements. When the majority of planets are in your western hemisphere, you are more altruistic. You will try to make decisions based on other people too.

STELLIA

Stellia are noted when three or more planets are found in the same house or the same sign.

They draw attention to the area of the horoscope in which they are found and can render this area of life, or mode of expression in the case of a sign, far more important than it would otherwise have been.

ASPECT PATTERNS

Aspect patterns are another good way to assess the combined influence of the birth chart as a whole. About half of birth charts have a recognizable pattern and many have more than one. Although their absence from a horoscope does not disadvantage, their presence is significant and should always attract your attention. Some aspect patterns pinpoint planets, houses or signs that are important whenever they are highlighted.

Many astrologers feel that a surplus of traditionally favorable aspects is not necessarily a good thing. Through difficulties we grow into complete and well-rounded individuals. The more stressful planetary combinations are often called dynamic, since through effort a change is implied and a better outcome can result. No one would wish for an excess of stress, but a little can be helpful for motivation.

T-SQUARE

The t-square is a potent combination of two planets in opposition, with a third planet square to them both. These are hard aspects, so the inherent potential is stressful, but varies widely in manifestation depending on which planets are involved. Channelling the potential of this configuration effectively means that much of its potential can be utilized for good. Related issues will always need to be addressed, but the difficulty with which this pattern is associated can, in theory at least, subsequently be dispelled.

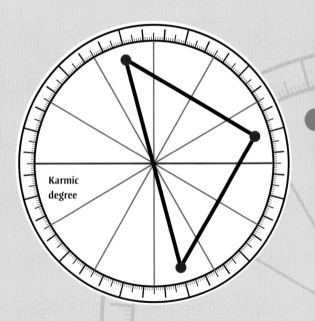

    The point in the horoscope opposite the apex of the t-square is sometimes called the karmic degree. It is toward the symbolism of this point that you should make your best efforts, judged according to the house and the sign placing in which this point is found. How easy or difficult this will be depends to some degree on whether the planets in the t-square fall mainly into cardinal, fixed or mutable signs. Mutable signs get around problems and cardinal signs face them head on, but those with the fixed quality predominant could find it harder making an impact.

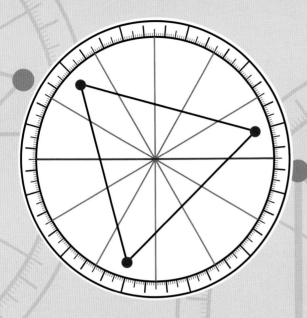

GRAND TRINE

A grand trine occurs when two planets are in trine aspect to one another, with a third planet trine to them both. Traditionally this is a very lucky pattern, linked with happiness, stability, good fortune and success, although more dynamic placings help bring out its best effects. Life can seem too easy otherwise, although strangely those difficulties that do occur are often felt acutely.

Where squares and crosses are organized by quality, trines are classified by element. Those with fire and air grand trines are fortunate through their own efforts, those with grand trines in earth and water have good fortune come to them. Mixed varieties of grand trine are usually termed *dissociate*.

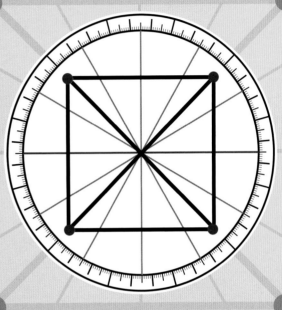

GRAND CROSS

Traditionally the most challenging of patterns, characterized as a cross to bear. The grand cross has two oppositions at right angles, with four interlocking squares to complete the picture. As with t-squares, you can classify a cross by quality and, again, fixed crosses are the most demanding.

Although there are many examples of those with grand crosses enjoying active, successful and fulfilling lives, there are many others for whom life has not exactly been fun. Real tragedy might not be indicated, but a grinding sense of underachievement, relationship disappointment and personal dissatisfaction is a heavy burden for anyone to live with in the longer term. The enclosed nature of this configuration can be trying, too, but some are more blessed than others with escape routes elsewhere.

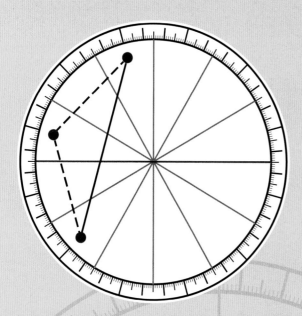

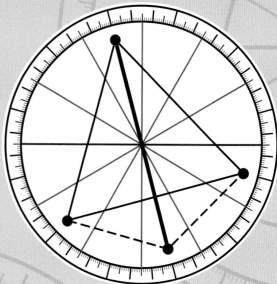

MINI GRAND TRINE

The mini grand trine has two planets in trine aspect, with a third planet in sextile to them both. This pattern occurs in either active or receptive signs, although it may become dissociate with allowable aspect orbs. As the name suggests, it is similar to a grand trine, but is of reduced influence. It is less important to seek compensatory challenges, since effort is already implied by the twin sextiles.

KITE

On the face of it, the luckiest pattern of all, as both the grand trine and mini grand trine formations are combined, but with the dynamic addition of a central opposition. Kites can be active or receptive, with a further dissociate form. The difficulty implied by the central opposition brings out the best from this configuration, although there is always some benefit to be derived from harder influences elsewhere. Without the need for change, the kite formation effortlessly drifts through life. You'll enjoy a happy, peaceful and easy time, but are you fulfilling your amazing potential?

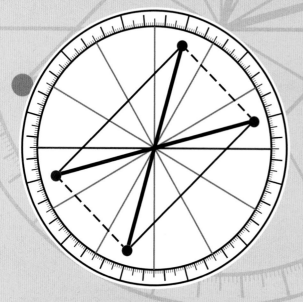

MYSTIC RECTANGLE

Four planets are connected by two parallel trines and two parallel sextiles, with two diagonal oppositions to give this structure and support. The mystic rectangle does not necessarily confer any mystical tendencies, although it may with some planetary combinations. It does occupy a large area of the chart, though, and comprises a good combination of harmonious and more dynamic influences, contained either within mainly masculine or mainly feminine signs.

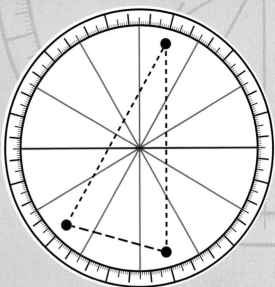

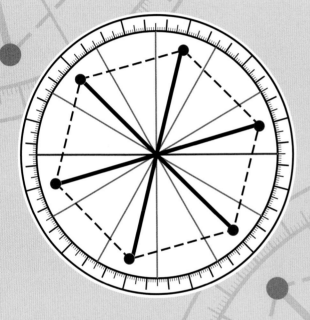

YOD

Two planets in sextile are both separately inconjunct a third. This is not strictly a major configuration, but is of major importance and is definitely worth investigating. It is sometimes called the Finger of Fate, or even the Finger of God. It points out a certain planet, the potential of which it is crucial to express. Initially, there is only a vague awareness of how important this is, but as time goes by it becomes more and more obvious. Times of crisis and despair herald important changes, leading on to transformation and a better outcome in the end.

GRAND SEXTILE

This is a rare but unmistakable pattern, with a clear hexagon made up of six evenly distributed planets forming six interlocking sextiles around a complex internal pattern. Grand sextiles will in principle occur in either masculine or feminine signs. While they do not seem to inspire either great ambition or material good fortune, a happy and fulfilling life can nonetheless be anticipated.

PUTTING IT TOGETHER 1

Holly was born at 4:30 p.m. in Wimbledon, south London, on Christmas Eve 1931. She has her Sun in Capricorn and the Sixth House, her Moon in Gemini and the Twelfth, with Cancer rising and Pluto in her First House.

CHART SHAPE

This horoscope has see-saw tendencies. Five planets clustered around the descendant place an emphasis on partnership affairs and roughly oppose the more self-deterministic energies of the eastern hemisphere. A self-versus-others dilemma ensues, which is sure to cause conflict in close associations. Individuality and the perceived needs of other people will have to be balanced for a peaceful life.

PLANETARY DISTRIBUTION

The quadrants are as equally represented as possible, as are the northern and southern hemispheres. There is a slight bias toward the western hemisphere, with a stellium of three planets in the Seventh House, showing that close relationships will certainly be a major draw. A stellium of four planets in Capricorn places an enormous emphasis on this sign. Capricorn characteristics, both for good and ill, are notable.

ASPECT PATTERNS

Saturn in Capricorn and the Seventh House opposes Pluto in the First House and Cancer. Both square Uranus in Aries and the Tenth House to form a cardinal t-square. Holly is a powerful character and is slow to trust. She is an extreme individualist who is not willing to tolerate any form of control. She is reluctant to form new relationships or to accept any binding personal commitments. Once involved she is dutiful, but feels trapped and then tries to break away. Not always acknowledging this drive for freedom, provocative and inflammatory behavior helps to precipitate a showdown. Holly's karmic degree is in the Fourth House and Libra, so she needs to seek balance within herself for true harmony ever to prevail in the domestic sphere.

SUN

Holly is a worker with her Sun in the Sixth House and Capricorn. She likes to feel busy and often worries about her health. Her outlook is serious, but is enlivened by Mercury in Sagittarius, which helps encourage a broader range of interest. The Sixth House combines with a trine to Neptune in the Second House. Holly tries to help out financially in times of trouble and could easily make money through creative or artistic pursuits. The connection between Mercury, Sagittarius, writing and publishing reinforces this theme, although the retrograde nature of Mercury is easily subjugated to preconceived ideas of responsibility.

MOON

Holly should have been a writer. With the Moon in Gemini, her need to communicate is palpable. Lunar oppositions to the conscious forces of the Sun and Mercury in the dutiful Sixth meant such frivolity could not be allowed. Similarly, a genuine emotional response is kept firmly under wraps. Holly very much needs emotional reassurance but feels that this will not be forthcoming. Better then to have a hard exterior than to end up being hurt.

ASCENDANT

The Ascendant is early in Cancer, so it is mainly this sign that occupies the First House. First impressions are tempered by Pluto, with attack becoming the best means of defence. Mars conjunct the descendant in Capricorn confers an often confrontational style, with the square from Uranus adding wilfulness and eccentricity. Some sensitivity comes from Neptune sextile to Holly's ascendant, but she is not somebody most people would want to mess around with!

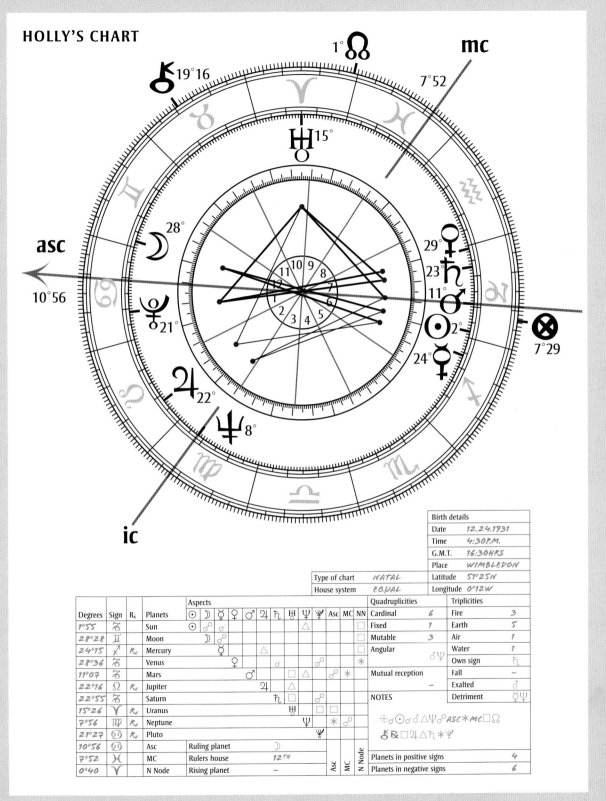

HOLLY'S CHART

Chart markings:
- 1° ♋ (N Node)
- mc 7°52
- ♂ 19°16
- ⛢ 15° (Uranus)
- asc 10°56
- ☽ 28° (Moon)
- ♀ 29°
- ♄ 23°
- ♂ 11°
- ☉ 2°
- ☿ 24°
- ⊗ 7°29
- ♇ 21° (Pluto)
- ♃ 22° (Jupiter)
- ♆ 8° (Neptune)
- ic

Inner houses numbered: 11 10 9 8 / 12 7 / 1 6 / 2 3 4 5

Birth details

Date	12.24.1931
Time	4:30 P.M.
G.M.T.	16:30 HRS
Place	WIMBLEDON

Type of chart	NATAL	Latitude	51°25N
House system	EQUAL	Longitude	0°12W

Aspects table

Degrees	Sign	Rx	Planets	☉	☽	☿	♀	♂	♃	♄	♅	♆	♇	Asc	MC	NN
1°55	♑		Sun	☉	☍	♂			△							□
28°28	♊		Moon		☽	☍										□
24°15	♐	Rx	Mercury			☿			△							□
28°36	♑		Venus				♀	♂				☍			✶	
11°07	♑		Mars					♂	□ △			☍	✶			
22°16	♌	Rx	Jupiter						♃	△						
22°55	♑		Saturn							♄	□		☍			
15°26	♈	Rx	Uranus								♅	□	□			
7°56	♍	Rx	Neptune									♆	✶	☍		
21°27	♋	Rx	Pluto										♇			
10°56	♋		Asc	Ruling planet	☽											
7°52	♓		MC	Rulers house	12TH											
0°40	♈		N Node	Rising planet	–											

Quadruplicities

Cardinal	6
Fixed	1
Mutable	3
Angular	
Mutual reception	–

NOTES:
⛢ ☉ ♂ ☌ ☽ △ ♆ ♂ ASC ✶ MC □ ☊
♂ Rx □ ♃ △ ♄ ✶ ♇

Triplicities

Fire	3
Earth	5
Air	1
Water	1
Own sign	♄
Fall	–
Exalted	♂
Detriment	☿ ♆

Planets in positive signs	4
Planets in negative signs	6

CHAPTER 5

INTERPRETING YOUR PLANETS

RISING AND RULING PLANETS

Not everybody has a rising planet. An approximation would be around 15 percent, but this is entirely subjective. The lack of a rising planet is not disadvantageous, but if you do have one, it's important. Its strength is such that it can outshine, or at least substantially modify, the sign on your ascendant.

A rising planet must be conjunct with your ascendant—that is to say, no more than eight degrees away. It can be in your Twelfth or First House, with the latter the most visible in personality terms. If you have more than one planet within this range, then, regardless of house placing, it's the one closest to your ascendant that is rising. If you have two planets exactly the same distance away, take the faster-moving one as your choice.

If you have no planets conjunct with your ascendant, you do not have a rising planet. You can only have one—any planets conjunct the ascendant apart from the closest are termed angular.

Your ruling planet is the planet that rules your ascending sign. Thus with Leo rising, your ruling planet is the Sun, and with Cancer rising, your ruling planet is the Moon. Even if your ascendant is very late in a sign, it's the sign it is found in that determines your ruling planet. Thus Venus rules the charts of those born with Taurus or Libra rising and Mercury rules the horoscopes of those with Gemini or Virgo on their ascendant. Everybody has a ruling planet!

Once you have established your ruling planet, the most important thing to note is the house in your birth chart in which it is found. This denotes a particular area of growth for you, in the manner of the planet concerned.

YOUR RISING PLANET

SUN

You are a big character with a sunny disposition. When you walk into a room everybody knows you're there.

MOON

You are nurturing, caring and relate to people on an emotional level. You are sensitive, receptive and reflective.

MERCURY

You're a chatterbox and you get bored easily. You need constant stimulation and are always on the go.

VENUS

You hate arguments. Be well-dressed, amenable and aim for an easy life, that's your ideal.

MARS

You are assertive, demanding and often confrontational. You could be competitive or cooperative, depending on how you feel.

JUPITER

You might be physically large, or have a big personality. You are optimistic and outgoing, but can't stand pettiness.

SATURN

You always look so serious. You might be having a great time, but nobody can tell.

URANUS

There is something remarkable about your appearance. You are good with computers and love the latest technology.

NEPTUNE

You are a master of glamour and illusion. For some you hold a strange fascination, others just think you're unreliable.

PLUTO

You try not to give much away. You have a strong personality and a quiet intensity. You may plot and scheme in secret.

YOUR RULING PLANET

SUN

You will develop most by being yourself, by letting your light shine and your inner child play.

MOON

You need to develop a warmer and more emotional response, trusting less to logic and more to your feelings.

MERCURY

You should develop your analytical abilities, your powers of reason, intellect, logic and observation. Encourage thought and communication, discourse and debate, wherever you can in your life.

VENUS

You need to establish and maintain peace, harmony and good relating in the areas of your life that are implicated. This doesn't mean just being a doormat, though.

MARS

Do not be afraid to assert yourself. It is important to consider others, but their needs should not always be placed above yours.

JUPITER

Jupiter shows growth, so as your chart ruler it's a double indication. Expect learning, travel and broadened experience, connected with the house highlighted.

SATURN

You need to determine where you stand. In time, through patient and sustained effort, you can affirm your true position.

URANUS

Your individuality must be expressed. Otherwise, some disruption is experienced.

NEPTUNE

Your dreams are important. Especially where indicated by the house involved, you have a need to follow your bliss.

PLUTO

You go through many changes, but ultimately want to feel in control. This applies mainly to the house Pluto occupies.

UNASPECTED PLANETS

An unaspected planet is one that doesn't aspect any other planet. This means that a planet can still form aspects to the angles, node, Chiron or the Part of Fortune and still function as unaspected. Such contacts are of reduced significance when no other planet is involved.

An unaspected planet can also form minor aspects, without compromising its unaspected status. This could even apply to something like a yod, where the focal planet would have enormous significance, because of this unusual double emphasis.

It used to be thought that unaspected planets were somehow weakened, since some contact with other planets and hence full integration into your personality was believed essential for the manifestation of a planet's full potential. Increasingly, though, astrologers have recognized that as a direct consequence of this lack of integration, the potential of an unaspected planet is enormously enhanced, but is always to some degree just beyond your control.

As well as having the potential for both a constructive or less constructive expression, unaspected planets work very strongly most of the time, but then suddenly by turns seem not to function at all. Sometimes, as well, you'll see two planets aspecting one another, yet neither are connected with anything else. This has been called an unaspected duet, where both planets demonstrate powerful characteristics that are beyond the subject's control.

You cannot help but strive to understand, anticipate and embrace any unaspected features in your horoscope. Such an emphasis and constant focus has been linked with special talents, in areas often signalled by the planet itself.

The Sun, Moon and Saturn are all unaspected in this birth chart. Most horoscopes do not have any unaspected planets, so to find this many in one person's chart is extremely rare.

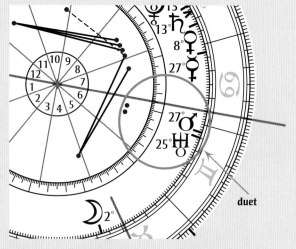

In this chart, Mars and Uranus are conjunct one another, but are not aspected by anything else. Such an unaspected pairing is called a duet.

YOUR UNASPECTED PLANETS

SUN

Much of your time is spent finding out who you are. You appear confident and creative, but inside feel completely the opposite. Women can have trouble with the men in their lives, beginning with the paternal influence and continuing into adulthood. You will need to balance strength with receptivity in your potential partners and until then veer between the two.

MOON

Your emotions are strong and need acknowledgment, but this powerful expression coexists with a colder and more calculating approach. A difficult experience of your maternal figure leads to issues surrounding domesticity and nurturing. Relationships with women, especially for men, can be fraught.

MERCURY

You are rather bright, but this can lead to loneliness and isolation from your peers. Usually rational, reasonable and communicative, on occasions you stun everyone with a spectacularly illogical decision. Similarly, either you never stop talking or you won't say anything at all.

VENUS

Venus governs love and security and, when unaspected, your attitudes to both fluctuate. One minute you are madly in love, the next you couldn't care less. On a whim you destroy situations that might have taken years to build. You hate arguments and confrontation, yet seem regularly to encounter both.

MARS

You are assertive and aggressive, so do well in the business world, where your competitive nature finds a positive outlet. Your energy can fluctuate, although you have more drive than most and you might lack patience and tolerance while you lay down the law.

JUPITER

Your personal appetites are enormous and you don't know where to stop. You want to learn about the world, you are keen to encounter your fellow man and you are probably very popular. You are mostly optimistic, exuberant and tolerant, yet at times feel strangely dejected as your confidence and enthusiasm evaporate.

SATURN

Although you seem calm and in control, you feel very different inside. Saturn governs structure and self-discipline, so when unaspected you are pedantic over the smallest issues, but then seem not to care about much bigger things. You ask for advice but don't listen.

URANUS

Individuality is the issue here, so most of the time you're a law unto yourself. Nobody can understand why someone as capable as you then gets into awkward situations through overcompromise.

NEPTUNE

You're idealistic, intuitive, spiritually oriented and creative. Sometimes you seem confused, unclear and impractical, while at others you try to kid yourself that life is purely black and white.

PLUTO

You are a control freak, with a sharp eye on everyone, and nothing can escape you. You enjoy a good battle and respect a stronger will, so can be surprisingly amenable with those you fear.

OTHER PLANETARY POSITIONS

At this stage in your interpretation, you should consider those planets implicated previously, but which were not emphasized sufficiently to concentrate on before. You must remember to bring in every planet at this stage.

Much of the real skill lies in prioritizing this information, so the most important things are those that you will look at first. After planets emphasized by their involvement in the chart shape, aspect configuration and any stellia, those that aspect the Sun, Moon and ascendant should be the next on your agenda. Assess everything in the usual way, with the planet concerned, the house and sign position and any aspects made.

INTERPRETING RETROGRADES

Retrograde motion is worth noting where a personal planet is involved, or when three or more planets are retrograde in a single chart. It is reasonable to describe such a person as sensitive and intuitive, regardless of which planets are involved. A retrograde personal planet shows a reduction in the expression of this planet's characteristics, since much of its potential is directed within.

For example, Mercury retrograde might make you less talkative, but also a better strategist and a deep thinker. Venus retrograde might make you shy, but also someone who would emphasize an inner poise above all else. Thus retrograde planets can have helpful consequences, as well as the difficulty that is often described.

FINAL STAGES

At this point a few planets will remain for your assessment. You might like to consider those found in their own sign, in exaltation, fall, detriment or in mutual reception, or maybe those that are in aspect to the MC/IC. Usually you will find that, by this stage, very little has been left out.

INTERPRETING PLANETARY PLACINGS

Interpreting a planetary placing can be complex, just as you are. In a way an astrological interpretation is like your own unique DNA, an incredibly complex entity, individual and different for each of us and the embodiment of the precise blueprint for who we will turn out to be.

Chemically, DNA is composed of four much simpler molecules, called bases, that are common to everyone. Stylistically, it is the order in which these bases are strung together that goes to make you a unique person. Much the same applies in astrology, where smaller building blocks are put together to form a far more complex whole. But instead of bases, in astrology it is these four factors—house, sign, planet and aspect—that we use as our key.

- **Houses** Houses show areas of your life. They are *where* energy will manifest in your birth chart.

- **Signs** Signs show ways of being. They are *how* that energy will manifest.

- **Planets and angles** Planets and angles show energies within you. They show *which* energy we are talking about.

- **Aspects** Aspects are fine tuning. They show *modifications* to this raw energy.

Having established what each placing means and how it might be working, you can then start to see how this relates to other areas of the chart.

FOR EXAMPLE

Let's take an unfussy placing, Mars in the Sixth House.

Mars is energy, action, drive, assertion, initiative and sometimes anger, aggression and discord.

Sixth House is health, work, duty, obligation, responsibility, service to others.

Put these together and you get . . .

Mars/Sixth House You put a lot of energy into your work. You like to be the boss and might fall out with your colleagues. You could be a fitness fanatic. You like to jog and join a gym.

But how might this be expressed when Mars is in Taurus?

Taurus is steady, reliable, determined. You are fond of routines, comfort and stability.

Mars/Sixth/Taurus You work hard, take the long view and your efforts are steady and determined. You are less likely to be self-employed because you value your security.

When Mars is in Aquarius?

Aquarius is erratic, eccentric, modern and unconventional, an individualist and perhaps a loner.

Mars/Sixth/Aquarius You tend to work sporadically, but may be gifted with new technology. You like group work, but will probably be happiest when you are self-employed.

Or found in watery Cancer?

Cancer Your emotions have a big impact, with a love of domesticity and periodic moodiness.

Mars/Sixth/Cancer How hard you work depends on how you feel. Your health also suffers when you feel gloomy or discouraged. You might like to work from home.

Mars/Sixth/Aquarius trine Jupiter/Tenth/Gemini—Your distinctive, innovative and hard-working approach is helpful in furthering your ambitions.

Venus/Twelfth/Leo opposition Mars/Sixth/Aquarius—Your drive to succeed at work can make you unhappy at times, as you must drag yourself away from your more private pleasures.

PUTTING IT TOGETHER 2

Let's look at Holly's chart, to see how a consideration of those planets remaining might be applied.

On first examination, the chart shape emphasizes the five planets clustered around the descendant, with the majority in Capricorn, the Seventh House or conjunct with the dsc.

RELATIONSHIPS

Venus is the natural ruler of the Seventh House, so Holly is not a loner. She won't ever feel happy or complete without a close one-to-one association. The presence of Venus conjunct Saturn, both in Capricorn and the Seventh House, shows considerable reserve, but great loyalty and commitment once involved. With her traditional outlook marriage is probable, and with both Venus and Mars in this status-conscious sign, her ideal partner would be someone whose successes are apparent to all. It could be hard for such a partner to keep pace with Holly's demands, since she is volatile and challenging and lives life with a passion. A lack of response to her frequent provocations might be perceived as indifference.

An opposition of Pluto to Venus and Saturn points the way to some complex relationship scenarios. These will be subject to issues of subtle and more overt control, guilt, manipulation and dominance, with both sex and money potentially being used as a means of keeping the upper hand. Intimate relationships have a powerful sexual component, with the likelihood of some strange and obsessive scenarios. Jealousy and possessiveness feature strongly, but the reserve of Saturn and Capricorn keeps such things mainly on the inside, until the kind of transformative crisis with which Pluto is justly associated forces her to take a closer look.

SELF-UNDERSTANDING

Holly needs to understand herself very well to avoid getting into relationships that do her no good. The openness of Mercury in Sagittarius helps her to talk things through, although, since this falls in her Sixth House and opposite her Moon, there will certainly be a tendency to underestimate and undervalue her emotional affairs.

Nonetheless, from another perspective this is by no means all bad news, since both Mercury and the Sun form helpful trines to planets in the Second House, as does Mars in ambitious Capricorn. Jupiter assists enormously from a financial point of view, so while money may not necessarily stay in Holly's hands for very long, there will always be a safety net and sufficient to go around. A trine from Jupiter to Uranus in the Tenth House suggests self-employment and an unusual career, because with Jupiter in Leo and Uranus in Aries, it is unlikely Holly could ever flourish as an employee.

FINANCIAL AFFAIRS

Jupiter in the Second can show extravagance, although this is offset considerably by the caution and prudence of the strong Capricorn emphasis. Neptune in the Second House is not noted for practicality, so some degree of circumspection is definitely to be recommended in all Holly's financial affairs. Nonetheless, given helpful aspects, there is an acute intuitive perception of where financial opportunity lies. Creativity and imagination can be used to financial advantage and music, illusion, film, fashion and glamour could all feature prominently. Many with Cancer ascending and Pisces on the Midheaven choose not to go out to work at all, preferring to stay home perhaps with their children or animals.

The conjunction of Neptune with Holly's IC is the closest aspect to exactitude in her whole chart. It shows how idealistic she is where her home life is concerned and how keenly any imperfections will be felt. Holly would enjoy living beside water or in the countryside, and with her five retrograde planets will always benefit from periods of seclusion. It is doubtful that any situation could ever equate truly with perfection, so she will need to realize that real peace and happiness ultimately come from within.

HOLLY'S CHART

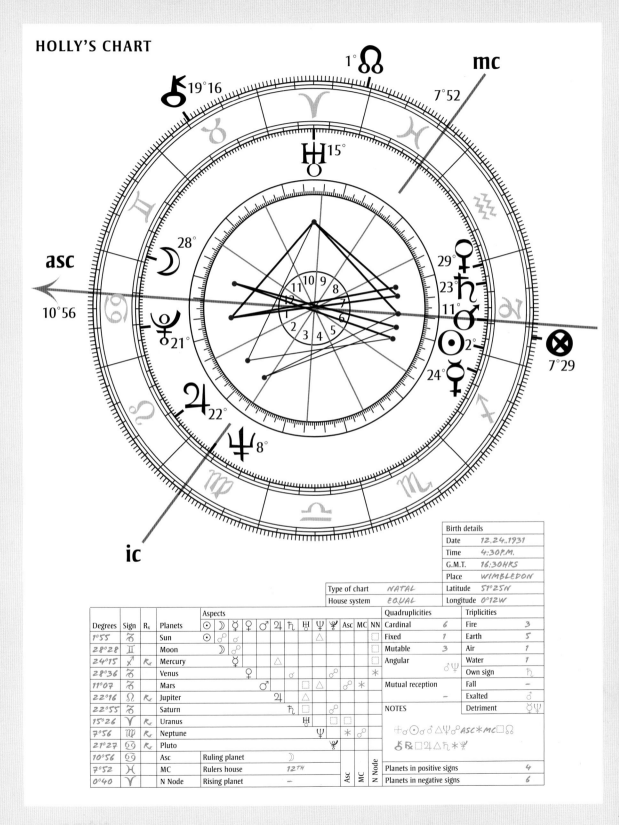

asc 10°56

mc

ic

Birth details	
Date	12.24.1931
Time	4:30P.M.
G.M.T.	16:30HRS
Place	WIMBLEDON

Type of chart	NATAL	Latitude	51°25N
House system	EQUAL	Longitude	0°12W

Degrees	Sign	Rₓ	Planets	Aspects															Quadruplicities		Triplicities	
				☉	☽	☿	♀	♂	♃	♄	♅	♆	♇	Asc	MC	NN						
1°55	♑		Sun	☉	☍	♂			△								Cardinal	6	Fire	3
28°28	♊		Moon		☽	☍											Fixed	1	Earth	5
24°15	♐	Rₓ	Mercury			☿			△								Mutable	3	Air	1
28°36	♑		Venus		♀			♂			☍			✱			Angular		Water	1
11°07	♌		Mars				♂		□	△		☍	✱						Own sign	♄
22°16	♌	Rₓ	Jupiter					♃		△							Mutual reception		Fall	–
22°55	♑		Saturn						♄	□		☍				–		Exalted	♂
15°26	♈	Rₓ	Uranus						♅	□	□					NOTES		Detriment	☿♆
7°56	♍	Rₓ	Neptune							♆	✱	☍							
21°27	♋	Rₓ	Pluto							♇						☿♀⊙♂△♆□ASC✱MC□☍			
10°56	♋		Asc	Ruling planet		☽										♑Rₓ□♃△♄✱♆			
7°52	♓		MC	Rulers house		12TH						Asc	MC	N Node	Planets in positive signs	4		
0°40	♈		N Node	Rising planet	–										Planets in negative signs	6		

113

SPECIAL FEATURES

MOON'S NODES

The celestial dynamics of the moon's nodes were discussed in Chapter 1. From an interpretative perspective they make up the first of a handful of overview techniques, which will help you to finalize your delineations from a holistic standpoint, in much the same way as you began.

THE NODES AND KARMA

The significance of the nodes leads quickly into unquantifiable realms. Many astrologers accept a link with karma, beginning first with large-scale events over which we have no control—for example, mass unemployment, war, famine, earthquakes or other natural catastrophes. If you are caught up in such events, is that just unlucky, or is it your karma to be born and there at this time? We all have our own beliefs and opinions, but from a quantifiable perspective, it's impossible to prove.

Other astrologers take things further and say that your nodal axis defines perfectly your entire spiritual purpose during this life, illustrating the issues you are bringing with you and those you must aspire to develop further. The concept of reincarnation and the details of who decides what is right for you must be taken as given, but most agree that

behind everything lies a central force, intelligence or, for many, a God. Nothing happens without a reason, although this can be almost impossible for us to accept and to appreciate at times. As mystics have always stated, and as Julian of Norwich emphasized back in the Middle Ages,

"... all shall be well and all shall be well and all manner of thing shall be well."

THE NODES AND REINCARNATION

In order to attain this perspective, the theory goes, we must reincarnate many times, living many lives and each time learning the lessons inherent in our birth chart. This helps astrologers to explain why some of the kindest, most innocent and blameless people die painful and premature deaths while many more miserable miscreants just go on and

North node

South node

on. It makes sense if we can say that really we live elsewhere, on a higher plane or what you will, put on the physical body as our diving suit and only stay here for so long as is needed to learn the lessons inherent in our chart.

The Moon's south node shows what you are born with, or, from a more psychological perspective, the types of behavior and reactions that come most naturally to you. The north node, assessed according to its house and sign position, shows those qualities you must develop as you mature and grow, whether for your spiritual betterment or simply to feel happier as a person. Since the north node and the south node are by definition in opposition, it is something of a struggle for us to reach our north nodal potential. This can be helped or made more difficult by other aspects, where a stellium of planets around your south node will have a tendency to impede your progress and a conjunction to the north node will help to pull you forward, for example. Softer aspects to your north node help to guide along; a square to one end of this axis is also a square to the other, so can effectively paralyze, since the subject is challenged both by the concept of spiritual growth and of maintaining the status quo. Sextiles to the north node are a mixed blessing, since some effort is implied to escape from the trine aspect that is inevitably formed by such a placing to your south node.

THE NODES AND SPIRITUAL PURPOSE

Your spiritual purpose might be surprisingly prosaic and focused on the material world. If your north node is in the Second House, then your karma is to learn to depend on your own resources, earning a living and making money for yourself. This may not sound very spiritual, but society would not go far without those who build the economy, pay their taxes, employ other people and help provide resources for the weak, sick and disadvantaged through their efforts. With this placing your south node is in the Eighth House, so your natural tendency is to look toward others for support. The more you learn to stand on your own feet, the happier you will be.

Whether you regard the moon's nodes as symbolizing your karmic and spiritual pathway, or simply believe that these are qualities within yourself that you must develop in order to feel happier and more complete, your north nodal direction is the one to aim for, assessed according to the house and sign in which the north node is found. Apart from this, the nodes can point toward self-development, communication, your family, partnership, learning, charity, your career, travel or anything else. You should develop their indications for true contentment, to go to bed feeling happy and to wake up feeling much the same.

INTERPRETING THE NODES

When it comes to understanding your nodes, the interpretations for a specific house placing are more or less interchangeable with that of the corresponding sign.

However, in practice you will usually be dealing with a blending situation, where, for example, the north node in Aries and the Seventh House shows the need to be more assertive in your closest relationships, since with your south node in Libra and the First House your natural tendency will always be to keep the peace. Inherently, you wish harmonious Libran principles to manifest through your outer personality.

Another example might be where your north node in Virgo and the Third House challenges you to analyze and to consolidate your ideas, rather than floating aimlessly around your South Node in an endless sea of inferred Piscean half-truths. With your north node in Pisces/Ninth and your south node in Virgo/Third, then the opposite is true and you will need to forget some of that excess Virgoan practicality.

NORTH NODE THROUGH THE SIGNS AND HOUSES

ARIES/FIRST HOUSE
♈ You are coming from a relationship perspective. With your south node in either Libra or the Seventh House, you put partnership matters first. You need to concentrate more on your own self-projection and should allow yourself to shine.

GEMINI/THIRD HOUSE
♊ You need to be accountable and to communicate. With your south node in Sagittarius or the Ninth House, you naturally would rather gallop away at the first sign of contradiction. You need to play your part in society.

TAURUS/SECOND HOUSE
♉ With your South Node in Scorpio or the Eighth House, taking a philosophical perspective comes naturally. You should work on the realization of those things you most value and should depend wherever you can on your own resources.

CANCER/FOURTH HOUSE
♋ With your north node in Cancer or the Fourth House, it is important that your domestic situation is not neglected. You are very responsible and focused on practicalities, but this could mean little without a more nurturing outcome.

LEO/FIFTH HOUSE

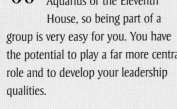

Your south node is in Aquarius or the Eleventh House, so being part of a group is very easy for you. You have the potential to play a far more central role and to develop your leadership qualities.

VIRGO/ SIXTH HOUSE

As you move from a nebulous Twelfth House or Piscean perspective, you accept responsibility for your work and physical health. While clarifying your position as Virgo demands, escapism and gullibility become things of the past.

LIBRA/ SEVENTH HOUSE

You must concentrate on your relationships and the achievement of more harmonious personal interaction. Since your south node is in either Aries or the First House, the talent for closer cooperation is a skill you could usefully acquire.

SCORPIO/ EIGHTH HOUSE

With your south node in Taurus or the Second House, you might focus excessively on the material world. You should emphasize less tangible but more universal values, and could try learning to share.

SAGITTARIUS/ NINTH HOUSE

With your south node in Gemini or the Third House, it is easy to fill up your days with rushing around. Unless you take time to develop your higher mind, though, you may end up wondering what you have achieved.

CAPRICORN/ TENTH HOUSE

Your natural tendency is to stay home, to keep out of the limelight and to put your family first. Fulfillment comes through the development of your career and by furthering your own aims more.

AQUARIUS/ ELEVENTH HOUSE

Being the center of attention comes naturally to you, but it is lonely and isolating always to be in charge. You don't necessarily need to sacrifice your individuality in order to be part of the team.

PISCES/ TWELFTH HOUSE

Since your south node is in Virgo or the Sixth House, you are preoccupied with mundane practicalities. Your north node encourages you to dream, to follow your ideals and your intuition.

PART OF FORTUNE

The origins and calculation of the Part of Fortune have already been discussed. From the perspective of interpretation this point shows pure joy and happiness, those activities that bring us the greatest pleasure and that help us to feel positive and glad to be alive.

As with the nodes, there is a considerable similarity between house placements and their corresponding sign positions. These are given together, but in practice you will usually be dealing with a blending situation. For example, your Part of Fortune in the Twelfth House and Gemini could mean that you are happiest on your own with time to think. Your Part of Fortune in the Eighth House and Cancer means that you are happiest when sharing your home with somebody else.

THE PART OF FORTUNE THROUGH THE SIGNS AND HOUSES

ARIES/FIRST HOUSE

♈ You need to be noticed, recognized and appreciated. You are happiest when making your mark. You aren't at your best when kept in the background and greet life with verve, energy and enthusiasm.

TAURUS/ SECOND HOUSE

♉ You are never happier than when making money, earning a living and building your security. This might sound a touch materialistic, but it is great if you are doing something you really enjoy.

GEMINI/THIRD HOUSE

♊ You are restless and easily bored. Your car and your telephone are your favorite possessions. You are happiest with plenty of variety and interesting people and with lots of different things to see and do.

CANCER/FOURTH HOUSE

♋ You love to stay home. Quiet nights in are your favorite thing. You like to care for and to look after people, with a soft spot for gardening, animals, children and your family.

LEO/FIFTH HOUSE

♌ You're a natural performer, at your best when center stage before your adoring public. Seriously though, you have a creative streak, could make a great teacher and are happiest when expressing yourself.

VIRGO/ SIXTH HOUSE

♍ You love to feel useful and get a warmer glow than most from a healthy lifestyle. You put duty before pleasure and feel contented when you have finished your daily chores.

LIBRA/ SEVENTH HOUSE

♎ Your idea of heaven involves pleasant surroundings, congenial company and sparkling social repartee. Some like a crowd, but most prefer a more intimate scenario. Love, culture and romance are the order of the day.

SCORPIO/ EIGHTH HOUSE

♏ You have an obsession with privacy and a love of solitude. You learn all you can about life's mysteries and about what motivates people. You know there is more to life than meets the eye.

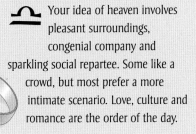

SAGITTARIUS/ NINTH HOUSE

♐ Travel broadens the mind, as do knowledge and wisdom, so their acquisition has much the same impact. You are drawn to faraway places and are always thinking of where you'd like to go next.

CAPRICORN/ TENTH HOUSE

♑ You are a serious and career-oriented person who sets a range of objectives for yourself. You are happiest when furthering your ambitions and when you have something important to do.

AQUARIUS/ ELEVENTH HOUSE

♒ You are goal-oriented, but focus more on intangible issues such as happiness and fulfillment than on more worldly matters like money and status. You're a sociable person and value your friends.

PISCES/ TWELFTH HOUSE

♓ You value your own space, are not afraid of your own company and have an active internal dialogue. The most significant events and revelations happen in your life when you are on your own.

CHIRON

The discovery and astronomy of Chiron have already been discussed. This is a recent addition for astrologers that has proven increasingly relevant over the past few years, despite its diminutive size, unusual features and distance away from the Earth.

THE CHIRON MYTH

Much of our current understanding is based around analyzing Chiron in classical mythology, where a connection is made between the symbolic nature of the ancient myth and current shared experience in our collective unconscious. For this same reason, it is thought no coincidence when a celestial discovery is named after a particular mythological figure or when the advent of such a discovery coincides with an upswing of interest in those matters with which it is linked.

In classical mythology, Chiron was a Centaur, with the head, arms and torso of a man and with the legs and the body of a horse. Chiron was rejected by his mother for his appearance, but despite this grew to become the esteemed tutor of kings and heroes, famous for being both gentle and wise. Chiron was renowned for his skills in the healing arts, but when he was accidentally wounded by a poisoned arrow, he was unable to cure his own pain. In desperation he gave up his physical immortality for that of a different sort, to be placed in the sky forever as the constellation of Sagittarius.

THE WOUNDED HEALER

The concept of the wounded healer proves central to understanding Chiron's impact. Chiron is best interpreted by house placement, showing an area in which you have experienced hurt and rejection, but where as a consequence you have the potential to blossom both in wisdom and maturity. Chiron's sign placing helps show how you can achieve this, but at up to eight years in every sign, such influences may be less specific.

Overall, Chiron helps us to transform old wounds and disappointments into a source of strength, both for ourselves and for others too. It shows where we must rise above hurtful experiences and where apparent setbacks can actually turn out in our favor. Wherever Chiron is placed in your horoscope, disadvantage has the potential to become an enormous plus.

CHIRON THROUGH YOUR HOUSES

FIRST HOUSE
You may think yourself unattractive and not the son or daughter that your parents wanted. Time teaches you to appreciate your individuality and to learn that you are unique.

SECOND HOUSE
A traumatic early experience pulls the rug from under you. Through material adversity and hardship, you learn that the only lasting security comes from within.

THIRD HOUSE

Life did not encourage you to speak your mind or to think for yourself. Perhaps formal education was not a success, or has left you with a feeling that you aren't very bright.

EIGHTH HOUSE

Perhaps a resource that was rightly yours was denied you, which has taught you to stand on your own two feet. True sharing could be hard, which makes sex a complex issue.

FOURTH HOUSE

An unfortunate event in your early home life, possibly involving your mother, leads to a special understanding of how important it is to feel safe, loved and nurtured.

NINTH HOUSE

Somehow, you weren't encouraged to develop your higher mind or your own view of life. You can rectify this by traveling, meeting lots of different people and by learning all you can.

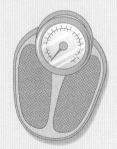

FIFTH HOUSE

The benefits of parenthood versus greater personal freedom could prove an important issue. This placing might indicate children, or perhaps your creativity as an expression of your own inner child.

TENTH HOUSE

From an early age your experiences with authority were discouraging, beginning possibly with a lack of support from your father. Healing comes as you further your ambitions and objectives for yourself.

SIXTH HOUSE

This can show health difficulties and the need consciously to improve your health routines. Sometimes your body is a source of distress and you must learn to accept yourself as you are.

ELEVENTH HOUSE

Ruling friends and your hopes and wishes, there could be challenging experiences with both. In time you learn the importance of friendship and the necessity of following your own course.

SEVENTH HOUSE

Close relationships have not always been the easiest. Gradually you develop an instinctive understanding of successful relating and are able to help others through their relationship difficulties.

TWELFTH HOUSE

Something, probably early on, has hurt you severely and at a fundamental level. By overcoming your insecurity, you develop a level of understanding most can only dream about.

CHART SIGNATURE

You have already recorded the distribution of the ten planets in your horoscope according to their position in signs categorized by one of the three qualities (cardinal, mutable or fixed) and one of the four elements (earth, air, fire or water).

Examine the table you filled out on pages 50–51 showing the number of planets corresponding to each quality and element in your birth chart. In most cases, you'll find that one quality and one element is dominant.

Combine the dominant quality and the dominant element to make a sign according to the following information. This sign is termed the chart signature.

If you can't establish a clear signature using just the ten planets, include the ascendant, midheaven, north node, Chiron and the Part of Fortune one at a time and in that order, until a clear dominance is achieved. Emma's chart, interpreted on page 128, is one such example. In this chart, all of these factors must be brought into the picture before the Gemini chart signature can be determined.

On rare occasions, no dominance will be apparent even then. The lack of a chart signature does not disadvantage you, but interpretation is easier when one can be found.

To interpret your chart signature, list as many positive traits of the chart signature sign as you can think of, prefaced by the phrase: "I would rather be more . . ."

Don't bother listing the less favorable characteristics of any sign since, as a rule, you won't aspire toward negativity.

UNDERSTANDING YOUR CHART SIGNATURE

Your chart signature represents your ego-ideal, the person you would most like to be. It shows qualities within yourself that you are trying to develop, although you may not recognize these initially and could be surprised by what is revealed. If your chart signature is the same as your Sun sign, you likely won't be surprised, since you already identify with these characteristics. If your horoscope has no chart signature, you may not have a clear idea of your ego-ideal, or perhaps your ideal combines the characteristics of more than one zodiac sign.

Effectively the chart signature acts as your conscience. When you fail to live up to your own expectations, it is what produces that guilty twinge and makes you feel less than happy with yourself. Since the chart signature reflects the overall balance of qualities and elements within your chart, once you become accustomed to what it is telling you, it usually feels quite natural to pursue these goals. The information below lists basic interpretations for the 12 chart signatures. Look out for your own special combination of quadruplicity and triplicity.

THE 12 CHART SIGNATURES

ARIES (CARDINAL FIRE)
You hate feeling dependent and so emphasize your strengths. You aim for autonomy and to be brave, adventurous, enthusiastic, active, spontaneous and direct.

TAURUS (FIXED EARTH)
You dislike inconstancy, but appreciate permanence and value stability. You would rather be more practical, patient, dependable and solid, cautious, affectionate and sensual.

GEMINI (MUTABLE AIR)

You feel you could communicate more logically and effectively. You try to be more versatile, adaptable, intelligent, lively, spontaneous, witty, talkative and bright.

CANCER (CARDINAL WATER)

You are longing to develop a more emotional response. You endeavor to be kind, protective, nurturing, sympathetic, tenacious, home-loving, thrifty and domesticated.

LEO (FIXED FIRE)

You like a central role. You are proud to demonstrate your leadership ability, or when you act in a noble and chivalrous way.

VIRGO (MUTABLE EARTH)

You are striving for a more practical approach. You are happy to be helpful, conscientious, modest, meticulous, systematic, diligent, orderly and neat.

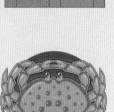

LIBRA (CARDINAL AIR)

A balanced and harmonious approach appeals to you. You aspire to be charming, cultured, elegant, smooth, suave, urbane and at peace with yourself.

SCORPIO (FIXED WATER)

You seek a greater persistence and to keep your own counsel. You cultivate depth, intensity, resolution, personal power, loyalty, subtlety, discernment and intuition.

SAGITTARIUS (MUTABLE FIRE)

You hope to greet life with greater tolerance and optimism. You are aiming to be more philosophical, positive, adventurous, confident, carefree and cheerful.

CAPRICORN (CARDINAL EARTH)

You aspire to greater self-discipline and to a more hard-working approach. You work at being ambitious, prudent, sensible, constant, determined, responsible and disciplined.

AQUARIUS (FIXED AIR)

Less repression and more expression is your theme. You favor a progressive outlook, an independent viewpoint, unconventionality, fairness and friendship.

PISCES (MUTABLE WATER)

Losing ego boundaries, you discover the urge to merge. You would rather be more charitable, caring and compassionate, receptive, intuitive, trusting and imaginative.

ANARETIC PLANETS AND VOID OF COURSE

Not all birth charts have an anaretic planet, but every horoscope has one that is void of course. In many ways the two terms are related, with an anaretic placing seeming to act as a more extreme expression of that which manifests in void of course.

ANARETIC PLANETS

An anaretic planet is one that has a position of 29°00 or greater in any sign. Most birth charts will not have an anaretic placing, but you can have one or several and the issues connected with this planet or planets will keep resurfacing throughout your life. Some astrologers note the final degree of Pisces particularly, since this is also the final degree of the zodiac.

With the Moon in an anaretic position, emotional issues are often to the fore. If the Sun is anaretic, there will be regular concerns over self-fulfillment and with being all you want to be. Neptune could show issues linked with your ideals and Pluto is associated with power and control, but by also considering these placings within the context of their sign and house position, even more information swiftly comes to light.

For example, with Mercury anaretic in Capricorn you need constantly to review your ambitions and career aspirations. If Venus is anaretic in the Eleventh House, then your friends are set to play a big part in your life. With an anaretic Mars in Aquarius and the Second House, the need to establish your own value system will prove paramount. With an anaretic Jupiter in the Fifth House and Sagittarius, it is going to take a while for you to settle down! As usual in astrology, the more attention you pay to the synthesis of your results, the more rewarding and detailed is your interpretation.

Think about the planet first—this is the part of you that will be primarily affected. Then consider the house and sign position in your chart to tell you where and how such issues will manifest themselves.

A planet found in the last degree of any sign is termed anaretic. Issues connected with this planet will regularly arise throughout a person's life.

OTHER FEATURES

Should you encounter an anaretic ascendant, remember that at the other end of one axis your descendant will also be anaretic, since issues involving how you present yourself cannot help but have an impact on your relationships too. Similar comments would apply to the MC/IC axis, where an uncertain direction makes it harder to fulfill your emotional needs, and problems with your career cause difficulties at home. The Moon's north node can be anaretic and, in such instances, your spiritual development is clearly to be emphasized. Chiron and the Part of Fortune can be anaretic too, emphasizing the principles of wounding and healing, together with the pursuit of happiness, in the charts of those concerned.

VOID OF COURSE

Working as a reduced version of an anaretic placing, your void of course planet is that with the highest degree placing regardless of the sign. If you have two planets at exactly the same position, it is the faster-moving one that you should choose. Your void of course (VOC) planet can also be anaretic, in which case a dual approach will apply in your interpretation. But whereas you might have any number of anaretic planets in your chart, you can only have one described as void of course.

Once you have determined your void of course planet, you need to work out the house it rules. For example, consider a birth chart with Saturn void of course. Saturn rules Capricorn, so where is Capricorn in your chart? In most cases you'll find it straddling two houses, but only one house will have a cusp in that sign. This is the one to note, since the affairs of this house will regularly prove irritating, not so severely as with an anaretic placing, but something you will notice nonetheless.

For example, with your void of course planet ruling your First House, you'll find often you don't seem to have come across as you had intended. If your void of course planet rules your Sixth House, you will have to pay more than average attention to your health.

OTHER FEATURES

With either Mercury or Venus void of course, you will have two houses highlighted, since Mercury rules both Gemini and Virgo and Venus rules Taurus and Libra. A void of course ascendant is probably valid, so long as you remember that this is actually the ascendant/descendant *axis* and regard rulership as of the First and Seventh Houses respectively. You can view the MC/IC axis in a similar way and give rulership to the Tenth and Fourth Houses, but won't be able to apply this technique to Chiron and the nodes, since establishing house rulership is impossible. The same comments are true of the Part of Fortune, although the pursuit of happiness will be of more than average concern for those with this feature highlighted.

PUTTING IT ALL TOGETHER 3

The concluding stages of Holly's analysis show how to interpret these special features. Having already decided on the main implications, strengths and challenges contained within your own birth chart, it is now time to make some important decisions.

A thorough analysis at this stage reveals ways in which to minimize difficulty and to address constructively your outstanding dilemmas. Ideally an overall course of expression can be established, by which to spur your further progress and guide your future self-development.

MOON'S NODES

Holly has her north node in Aries and her south node in Libra, so close relationships are extremely important. But this is a see-saw chart, with an undeniably strong pull toward individuality, which could prove troublesome if her own needs are not addressed.

This dilemma is highlighted by Holly's north node in Aries, showing that greater self-expression and a stronger sense of self are actually traits to develop. Holly needs to move away from the overcompromise of her south node in Libra and must embrace freedom of action as defined by Aries and the Ninth.

Holly could face an important decision regarding whether to live in the countryside or in a more urban situation, but as the Ninth House rules the country and the Third House rules the town, it is the rural option that should be preferred. There are challenges from the Sun, Moon, Mercury and the Part of Fortune to the furtherance of Holly's spiritual path, so she should be careful that the obligations of her closest associations and a tendency to repress her feelings do not hold her back.

PART OF FORTUNE

Holly's Part of Fortune is in the Sixth House and in Capricorn, so she is happiest when working. Fortunately this fits well with the Capricorn emphasis in her horoscope generally and is even conjoined by her Sun and Mars. A square from the Part of Fortune to her north node shows that what makes Holly happiest is not necessarily the best thing in terms of her spiritual development, when sometimes she might be tempted into sticking with oppressive liaisons and routines.

CHIRON

With Chiron in the Eleventh House, Holly would have received a setback to her hopes, most probably early in life and in a way that made her question the reliability of her friends. Chiron in Taurus square Jupiter in Leo and the Second House shows this was a substantial blow to her sense of self, which, with a trine to Saturn in the Seventh House, helped reinforce her opinion that relationships are almost more trouble than they're worth. However, with a sextile to Pluto in her First House of personality, such experiences have ultimately changed Holly for the better.

CHART SIGNATURE

With six planets in cardinal signs and five in earth, Holly's chart signature is clearly Capricorn, like her Sun sign. She is trying to be even more responsible and hard-working.

VOID OF COURSE

Holly doesn't have any anaretic chart features, but Venus is void of course and rules the Fourth and the Eleventh Houses. As sources of minor irritation for Holly, the Fourth House echoes the themes of Neptune conjunct her IC and emphasizes the difficulty in meeting her exalted expectations of that perfect home. Chiron in the Eleventh is a reminder that, although her fondest hopes and wishes may once have received a serious blow, the opportunity exists for a much more favorable outcome later.

HOLLY'S CHART

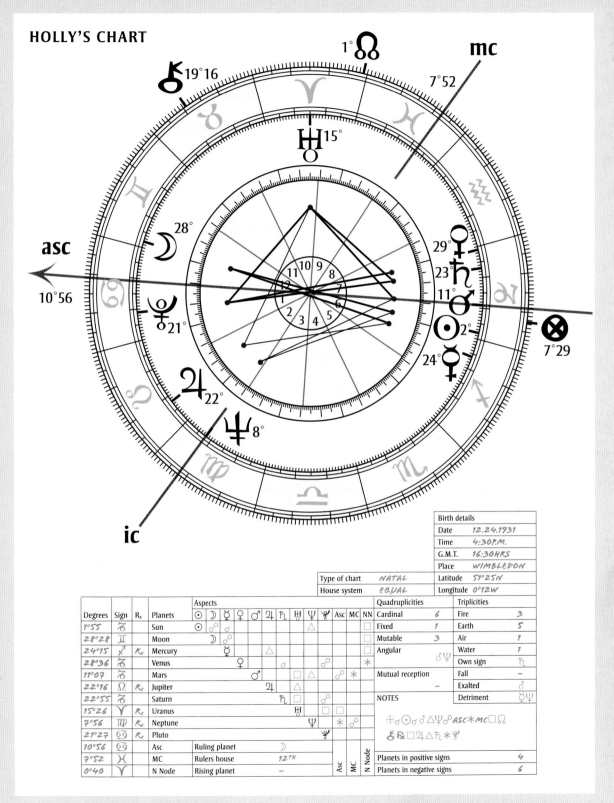

Birth details				
Date	12.24.1931			
Time	4:30 P.M.			
G.M.T.	16:30 HRS			
Place	WIMBLEDON			

Type of chart	NATAL	Latitude	51°25N
House system	EQUAL	Longitude	0°12W

Degrees	Sign	Rₓ	Planets	Aspects ☉ ☽ ☿ ♀ ♂ ♃ ♄ ♅ ♆ ♇ Asc MC NN	Quadruplicities		Triplicities	
1°55	♑		Sun	☉ ⚹ ☌	Cardinal	6	Fire	3
28°28	♊		Moon	☽ ⚹ ☌	Fixed	1	Earth	5
24°15	♐	Rₓ	Mercury	☿ △	Mutable	3	Air	1
28°36	♑		Venus	♀ ☌ ⚹ ⚹	Angular	♂♆	Water	1
11°07	♑		Mars	♂ □ △ ⚹ ⚹			Own sign	♄
22°16	♌	Rₓ	Jupiter	♃ △	Mutual reception		Fall	–
22°55	♑		Saturn	♄ □ ⚹	–		Exalted	♂
15°26	♈	Rₓ	Uranus	♅ □	NOTES		Detriment	☿♆
7°56	♍	Rₓ	Neptune	♆ ⚹ ⚹				
21°27	♋	Rₓ	Pluto	♇				
10°56	♋		Asc	Ruling planet ☽				
7°52	♓		MC	Rulers house 12TH	Planets in positive signs	4		
0°40	♈		N Node	Rising planet –	Planets in negative signs	6		

WORKING WITH ASTROLOGY

CASE STUDY: EMMA

Emma was born at 5:55 a.m. on Saturday, August 21, 1965, in a village called Cuckfield in the southeast of England. At the time of writing she is approaching forty, lives not far from where she was born, has four children from her first marriage and is married for the second time to a man 12 years her junior. Emma is currently working on her own beauty business, as well as caring for her family.

FIRST IMPRESSIONS

CHART SHAPE

This is a bucket chart, with a handle of Saturn in Pisces and the Seventh House, highlighting immediately Emma's central need for stable one-to-one relating. Although Saturn brings commitment and responsibility, it also introduces certain difficulties, so this journey is a hard one. Hard aspects to Emma's Moon and to planets in her First House show that although close relationships are vital, an entirely smooth passage will not be the case.

PLANETARY DISTRIBUTION

The first quadrant receives a powerful emphasis, containing six out of Emma's ten planets. This puts a strong focus on the self, a theme augmented by the presence of eight out of ten planets in the eastern hemisphere. Although the distribution of planets is more balanced between the north and south, a stellium of planets in the First House heightens the importance to Emma of her own desires, wants and needs. Traditionally she should seek balance elsewhere, but with Leo ascending and the Sun rising in its own sign, this may not be easy to find!

ASPECT PATTERN

There are three discernible aspect patterns in this chart. First, a mini-grand trine involving the Sun, Mars and Jupiter and second, two mutable t-squares that implicate the Moon, Saturn and Uranus in one instance and the Moon, Saturn and Pluto in the other.

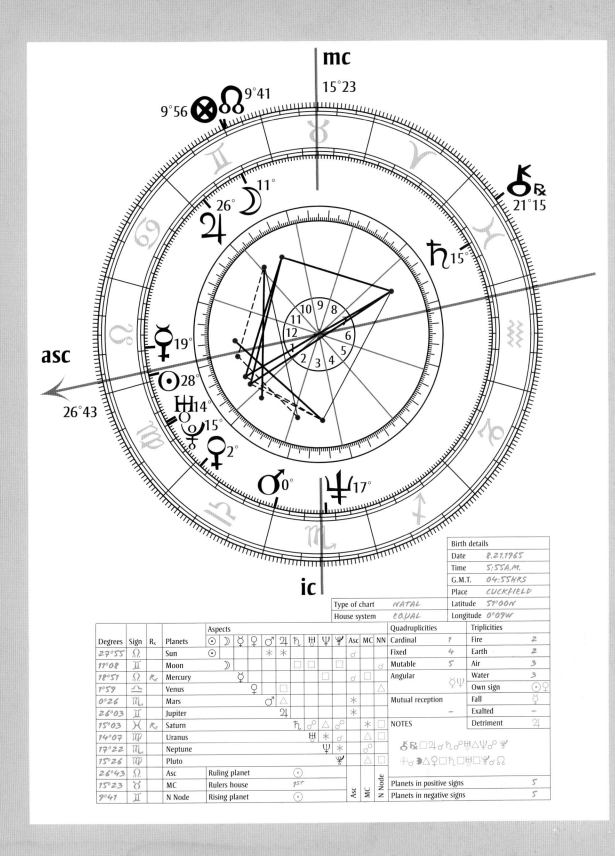

Birth details

Date	8.21.1965
Time	5:55 A.M.
G.M.T.	04:55 HRS
Place	CUCKFIELD

Type of chart	NATAL	Latitude	51°00N
House system	EQUAL	Longitude	0°09W

Degrees	Sign	Rx	Planets	Aspects ☉	☽	☿	♀	♂	♃	♄	♅	♆	♇	Asc	MC	NN
27°55	♌		Sun	☉				✳	✳					σ		
11°08	♊		Moon		☽			□	□		□					σ
18°51	♌	℞	Mercury			☿					□	σ	□			
7°59	♎		Venus				♀		□						△	
0°26	♏		Mars					♂	△		✳					
26°03	♊		Jupiter						♃		✳					
15°03	♓	℞	Saturn							♄	σ	△	σ	✳		□
14°07	♍		Uranus								♅	✳		△		□
17°22	♏		Neptune									♆	✳	σ		
15°26	♍		Pluto										♇	△		□
26°43	♌		Asc													
15°23	♉		MC													
9°41	♊		N Node													

Quadruplicities		Triplicities	
Cardinal	1	Fire	2
Fixed	4	Earth	2
Mutable	5	Air	3
Angular	☿ ♀	Water	3
		Own sign	☉ ♀
Mutual reception		Fall	☿
	–	Exalted	–
NOTES		Detriment	♃

NOTES: ♀℞ □ ♃ σ ♄ σ ♅ △ ♆ ☌ ♇
☌ ♂ ☽ △ ♀ □ ♄ □ ♅ □ ♆ ☌ ♇ ☌ ♋ ☊

Ruling planet	☉
Rulers house	1ST
Rising planet	☉

Planets in positive signs	5
Planets in negative signs	5

The mini-grand trine is a great boon. Both Mars and Jupiter form sextiles to the Sun, as well as a trine to one another. Emma is popular, likeable and outgoing with a natural exuberance, plenty of vitality and loads of energy. The trine between Mars and Jupiter shows initiative and good fortune, so is particularly helpful when starting new things. With Mars in her Third House and Jupiter in Gemini, she is never likely to run short of ideas, plus the added persistence of Mars in Scorpio helps her to see things through. Jupiter in the Tenth House means career matters should go well, given adequate application and with due regard to any interpersonal difficulties that might arise.

It is interesting that this helpful and positive configuration centers around the more conscious and immediately perceptible facets of Emma's personality, by focusing on her Leo Sun, Leo ascendant and her Sun rising in the First House. By contrast, on a deeper level the subconscious lunar influence suffers somber and much more stressful contacts, with squares to Saturn, Uranus and Pluto, all pinpointing complex and suppressed emotional issues harking back to early days. The lessons of Saturn in the Seventh House contrast starkly with the powerfully self-deterministic energies present elsewhere in this chart, making harmonious relating sure to be a very fraught issue indeed.

Until she can emphasize a Sagittarian approach to her Fourth House, the house and sign containing the karmic degree of both t-squares, interpersonal difficulties will impede Emma's successful pursuit of her broader aims and objectives. Sagittarian matters combine with the Fourth House to highlight an unconventional home life, with plenty of freedom necessary, but also with the need for a much greater awareness, openness and honesty regarding her true emotional concerns.

Some emotional repression is indicated by the Moon squares to both Saturn and Pluto, with such matters sure to be most problematic when their fundamental causes are not fully open to disclosure.

SUN
Many of the Sun's associations have already been discussed. With her Sun rising in Leo, Emma manifests Leonine characteristics in abundance. She is extravagant, likes to be the center of attention and is enormously fond of children and animals. She has a huge personality that you either love or loathe, since some might experience her bombastic manner as a little overbearing.

MOON
Lunar associations have also been considered via the aspect patterns in which they are involved. The Moon in Gemini stresses Emma's need to communicate. The Moon in the Tenth House shows the importance of her career, a difficult thing to accentuate while family responsibilities beckon.

ASCENDANT
Emma's ascendant is Leo, receives sextiles from Mars and Jupiter and conjunctions from Mercury and the Sun. She is sociable, a talker and not at her best when kept out of the spotlight or behind the scenes.

INTERPRETING THE PLANETS

RISING PLANET
The Sun is rising in Emma's horoscope. Its associations have already been discussed.

RULING PLANET
As well as rising, the Sun is also ruling this chart. This is unusual, so the associations of Leo and the Sun will be especially prominent.

UNASPECTED PLANETS
There are no unaspected planets in this chart.

MERCURY
Although Mercury is angular and conjunct with Emma's ascendant, making her talkative, outgoing and happy as the center of attention, it is placed in her hidden Twelfth House, so there's a lot that she keeps to herself. Leo usually confers an honest and straightforward attitude, but the square to Neptune could undermine her confidence when faced with those who seem stronger and more certain of their views. A square to the MC/IC axis means that the influence of others can potentially damage the Taurean stability that she craves. Subterfuge and deception are unfortunate consequences, should Emma feel her will cannot be expressed more directly.

VENUS
Venus is strongly placed in Libra and the Second House, the sign and the house that it rules. This emphasizes partnership and means that Emma won't be happy single. An attractive mate is essential, one who is suave, sophisticated and cultured in the finer things, with a bulging bank balance as an added bonus. A square to Jupiter could see Emma diving prematurely into new relationships, only later to repent at her leisure. A mate of a different age or background would be ideal.

MARS
Mars is in the Third House and Scorpio.
Its involvement in the mini-grand trine has already been discussed. Mars in the Third gives sharp intellectual and communicative faculties, but could lead to long-term grudges should more assertive impulses not find adequate expression.

JUPITER
Jupiter is in the Tenth House and Gemini and its aspects have already been discussed. Jupiter in this position bodes well for career matters and for the successful attainment of Emma's worldly objectives. Jupiter in Gemini is considered in detriment, since there might be a tendency to scatter her attention. Similarly, Jupiter's placing in the Tenth House can make matters a little too easy, when without additional incentive not so much is achieved as might otherwise have been hoped.

SATURN
Of pivotal importance, the influence of Saturn cannot be underestimated. Saturn in the Seventh House shows loyalty, but also the tendency to take on too much where relationships are concerned, and sometimes, eventually, to view the whole business as more trouble than it is worth. Venus in Libra and the Second House means that Emma will persevere, if only for the sense of security that a relationship gives her, but there are big dilemmas between this and her more assertive nature, as evinced by the Saturn oppositions to her First House and the square to her Moon in the Tenth. Luckily a trine to her Neptune/IC conjunction demonstrates how her committed approach to long-term associations helps to further her ideals for her home and family situation. A sextile to her MC in Taurus echoes this theme of perseverance and durability, if not exactly the prospect of fun.

URANUS

Uranus in Emma's First House shows an unusual person, a true individual, one who likes space and freedom and who won't appreciate being bossed around. A conjunction with Pluto shows a strong personality, one who despite her forthright nature keeps a lot to herself, with self-control very much in evidence astrologically, all of the time. Since this conjunction is in favorable aspect to Emma's MC, she might be surprised to find out that by letting go a little, further opportunities will come her way.

NEPTUNE

Neptune is conjunct with Emma's IC, so underneath is a sensitive person, one who desperately hopes that her emotional needs will be fulfilled, but who is very much afraid that this will not happen. Neptune in the Third House introduces a hint of sensitivity and promotes intuition, compassion and imagination, working well with the more assertive First House energies to bring greater balance. Unfortunately a lack of confidence can lead to confusion and subterfuge, so it will be important for Emma to communicate clearly and to make sure that her message always gets across.

PLUTO

Pluto in the First House has already been discussed. Jealousy and bitterness may build with this placing. Combined with Mars in Scorpio, it would be better not to make an enemy of Emma, unless you were prepared for the long haul. These placings give Emma the ability to keep her true feelings secret and not to allow her adversaries even the smallest advantage.

SPECIAL CHART FEATURES

MOON'S NODES

Emma's north node is in the Tenth House and Gemini. This places her south node opposite, in Sagittarius and the Fourth House, and so in developmental terms, Emma finds it easy to grow through her domestic and family affairs, since these are what she naturally favors to pursue. This is fortunate, since carefree optimism and a free self-expression at home have already been highlighted by the karmic degree of her two t-squares.

However, the north node in Gemini and the Tenth House adds another dimension, since it is clear that to neglect her career and personal ambitions entirely simply won't do. Gemini implies thought, so Emma needs to think about what she would like to achieve, then to focus and to stop herself from being distracted by the demands and opinions of others. With a Sagittarian south node she gallops away from problems, believing that things will be better in a different situation and with somebody else, while perhaps never really addressing the underlying issues. Although without doubt a home and family is important, it should not be an excuse to give up elsewhere. To withdraw to a safe base is wonderful; to run home whenever difficulty threatens probably is not.

Emma's Tenth House and Gemini Moon is conjunct her north node, emphasizing the importance of this nodal position and the dual t-squares that have been discussed. Squares to Saturn, Uranus and Pluto highlight the difficulties that Emma faces, trying to get along with people, at work especially. Luckily a trine to Venus in Libra helps enormously. She can be so charming when she wants!

PART OF FORTUNE

Emma's Part of Fortune conjoins her north node, with an orb of only fifteen minutes. Although Emma has her difficulties, she is also lucky in many respects. Here is one example, which will work as a powerful motivating force where her career aspirations and overall ambitions are concerned. After all, if what is good for you is also what makes you the happiest, you will naturally want to pursue this direction further. Aspects to her Part of Fortune are otherwise the same as to the north node, so similar comments, benefits and pitfalls apply.

CHIRON

Chiron is in the Seventh House and Pisces conjunct with Saturn, which as the handle of Emma's bucket formation started off this story. It would seem that a wounding experience occurred early in Emma's life, which has subsequently become internalized to set the tone for her adult relating. The conjunction to Saturn suggests her father was implicated and that the pain of such rejection has made her careful not to hurt others in the same way. This would explain Emma's tendency to stick with unfulfilling relationships long after their expiry date has clearly passed.

A trine to her Neptune/IC conjunction shows that in order to achieve the ideal nurturing home situation that she dreams about, Emma will need to work at these emotional concerns. The nature of Chiron means that in time she can not only heal herself, but also provide a solid support for others who may feel similarly lost and abandoned. Chiron squares Jupiter in her Tenth House and Gemini, so this will draw her focus away from more concrete, worldly and selfish ambitions. Periodic flare-ups will be characteristic when the need to concentrate on other people opposes the more self-assertive energies of Uranus and Pluto in her First House.

CHART SIGNATURE

Emma's chart signature is Gemini, but only after the ascendant, midheaven, north node, Chiron and the Part of Fortune have all been taken into account. Emma would rather be more logical, analytical and communicative, helping to defuse those complex emotional machinations that can only grow more troublesome the longer they are kept suppressed.

ANARETIC PLANETS AND VOID OF COURSE

Emma does not have any anaretic planets, although her Sun is void of course. In this horoscope where Leo is rising, the Sun rules the First House. Since the First House is Emma's interface with the world, it is this that proves a continuing source of irritation. It will show as she flies unexpectedly off the handle, when the weight of obligation, responsibility and all those little compromises that she hasn't mentioned becomes once more, for a moment, just too much to bear.

TAKING THINGS FURTHER

Astrology is a vast subject. A couple of birth charts down and your questions are just beginning. To whet your appetite for some of the other ways in which astrology is used today, let's finish by looking briefly at the forecasting of future trends, together with how to get the most from your closest relationships.

FORECASTING AND PREDICTION

TRANSITS

There are two main ways of predicting current and future trends astrologically. The first is based on the movement of the planets day to day and is known as planetary transits, or simply *transits* for short.

Your birth chart is a snapshot of the sky at the moment you were born, but all the planets keep moving, in effect around the fixed framework of your chart. Planets orbit at different speeds, with the outer planets the main focus of attention, since they pass slowly through the zodiac and have longer to exert a significant effect.

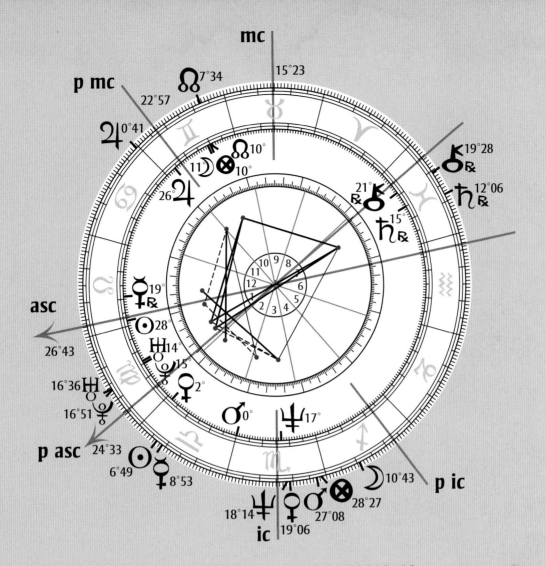

The planets still mean the same things as in your birth chart and so do the houses, but only for so long as each transit lasts. Thus working with transits is not too difficult, since once you have an ephemeris you can see where the planets are on any day you like. Often it is enough just to read off their placings at midnight and to plot them around the outside of your chart.

Take a look at the chart opposite to see where the planets are on Emma's fortieth birthday, for example. Saturn transiting her Twelfth House shows the end of a cycle, anticipating the slow rebirth of Saturn over her ascendant. Pluto in her Fourth House and Uranus in her Seventh both indicate changes at home, with unsettled relationships and a need to address the underlying issues.

PROGRESSIONS

This second method is more complex, since you need to calculate a new birth chart, for the same birthplace and GMT time, but one day later for every year of a person's life. So, if somebody is 20, you would count forward 20 days from their date of birth and cast a new chart. If they are 40, it's 40 days and for 60, you are counting forward for about two months. This new chart is your progressed horoscope for that year of your life and can be plotted around the outside of your birth chart, as shown above for Emma, aged 40.

You'll notice that unlike a transit chart, your progressed chart has a new set of angles. Both your natal and progressed angles are important, when contacting or being contacted by your natal or progressed planets. In Emma's chart, you'll

SYNASTRY

You'll already be familiar with superimposing one set of planetary positions on top of your birth chart. Now, instead of assessing the influences for a given moment in time, you'll be taking another person's birth chart to assess their impact on you.

Your interpretation should again emphasize planetary symbolism. Notice the houses relative to your own horoscope in which the other person's planets fall, since these will be the areas of life in which this person mainly affects you. For example, in the synastry between Holly and her husband, Mike, his Moon and Venus both fall in her Eleventh House, showing a relationship that is founded on friendship. Conversely, her Moon and ascendant in his Eleventh House help to confirm this theme.

The Moon and Venus are always important relationship planets. You can assess how they aspect the same points in a friend, colleague, partner or family member's chart. Even without looking for a precise aspect, you can quickly check out their relationship by sign. Seek harmonious mixtures that ensure understanding and support—for example, fire and air Moons go well together, or an earth Moon and a water Moon will work much the same.

Holly and Mike both have Moon in Gemini, so their Moons are in the same sign. Conjunct would be perfection, but otherwise things don't come a lot better!

notice the upcoming conjunctions of the progressed midheaven to her natal and progressed Jupiter as a very significant time, one where expansion, particularly in career matters, could be enormous and where Emma might be the only one setting limits for her progress. The MC/IC axis has a regular progression of about one degree per year, so with only a two-degree orb permissible for such protracted contacts, this influence will start to become apparent in around 12 months.

ASTROLOGY AND RELATIONSHIPS

Considering our relationships astrologically involves the application of two techniques. First, synastry, where the birth chart of one partner is superimposed onto the birth chart of the other. Second, the composite chart, where by averaging the natal placings of both partners a horoscope is made up for the relationship itself.

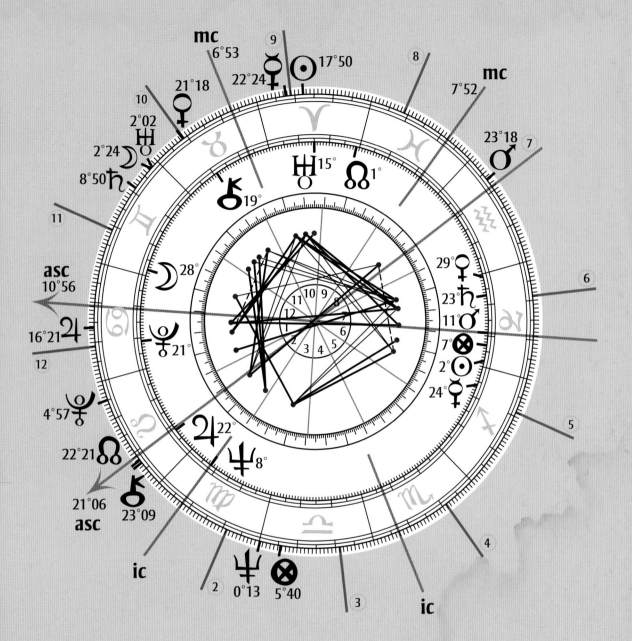

COMPOSITES

The composite chart is an average between two people's birth charts—say, for example, you and your partner. To average out two charts, convert each placing into absolute longitude, using the same methods you used to work out the Part of Fortune back in Chapter 1.

1 Add the Sun's degree position for one person to the Sun's degree position for the other and divide by two, finding what astrologers call the *midpoint* of this configuration, the position in the zodiac that lies halfway between the two.

2 Check that your answer is within 90 degrees of both natal placings, since this means you have found the shortest distance between them on the zodiac circle. If it isn't within 90 degrees, take the polarity sign from your answer at the next stage as your final position.

3 Convert back to the natural zodiac, repeat for every placing and then draw up the chart. A composite has no birth details and no retrogrades, since it is purely midpoints you are emphasizing.

The composite chart shows the character of the relationship itself, since once two people get together, an energy is generated that takes on a life of its own. You should look for helpful Fourth, Fifth or Seventh House energies in romantic relationship, for the Second, Sixth and Tenth Houses in a professional association and for the Third, Ninth and Eleventh Houses to be highlighted in a friendship. Holly and Mike's composite has a wonderful Seventh House stellium, although with Mars on their composite descendant, the sparks are known regularly to fly.

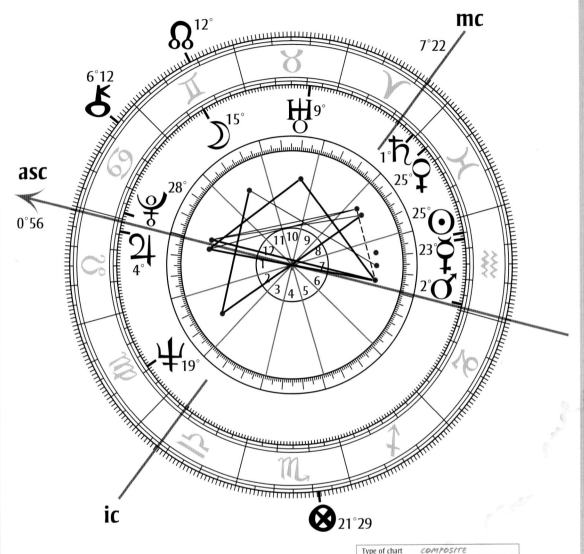

Degrees	Sign	Planets	Aspects														
			☉	☽	☿	♀	♂	♃	♄	♅	♆	♇	Asc	MC	NN
24°52	♒	Sun	☉				♂								
15°25	♊	Moon		☽						□					♂
23°19	♒	Mercury			☿										
24°57	♓	Venus				♀			♂		♂	△	△		
2°12	♒	Mars				♂	♂	∗	□		♂	♂			
4°19	♌	Jupiter						♃	△	□		♂	♂	△	
0°52	♈	Saturn							♄		△	△	△	♂	
8°44	♉	Uranus								♅					
19°05	♍	Neptune									♆				□
28°12	♋	Pluto										♇	♂		
0°56	♌	Asc	Ruling planet	☉											
7°22	♈	MC	Rulers house	7ᵀᴴ											
11°31	♊	N Node	Rising planet	♆											

Type of chart	COMPOSITE
House system	EQUAL

Quadruplicities		Triplicities	
Cardinal	2	Fire	2
Fixed	5	Earth	3
Mutable	3	Air	3
Angular	♂ ♃ ♄	Water	2
		Own sign	–
Mutual reception		Fall	♄ ♅
–		Exalted	☿ ♀
NOTES		Detriment	☉ ♆

NOTES:
♂□♄∗♅□mc
♃□☉⊙♀☿△♀∗♆△♇

Planets in positive signs	5
Planets in negative signs	5

GLOSSARY

angles The four orienting parts of your birth chart. Actually comprises two major axes, the ascendant/ descendant and midheaven/imum coeli.

angular Within eight degrees of any of the birth chart's angles. Conjunct with an angle.

ascendant The constellation rising in the east at the time and for the location of your birth.

aspect A geometric relationship between two chart features, which modifies the impact of the features concerned.

cardinal Term used to describe the signs of Aries, Cancer, Libra and Capricorn, according to characteristics that they share.

composite chart An amalgamation of the birth charts of two people, giving an equivalent chart for their relationship.

conjunction Term used to describe two chart features that are immediately adjacent in your horoscope. A separation of eight degrees is allowed.

cusp The boundary between two signs or two houses.

descendant The constellation setting in the west at the time and for the location of your birth.

detriment Traditionally a weaker placing for a planet, in the sign opposite from its rulership.

dignity Traditionally a strong placing for a planet, in the sign that it ordinarily rules.

element Fire, earth, air or water. A term used to categorize signs according to characteristics that they share.

ephemeris Plural: ephemerides. From the Greek word for diary, a source of reference that lists planetary positions on a regular basis, often daily.

exaltation Traditionally a strong placing for a planet, although perhaps the dignity is more favorable.

fall Traditionally a weaker placing for a planet, in the sign opposite from its exaltation.

fixed The signs of Taurus, Leo, Scorpio and Aquarius are all described as fixed. They are good organizers and don't give up easily, but can be very stubborn.

hard aspect Conjunctions, squares and oppositions are known as the hard aspects. Their energy is challenging, but has a lot of potential if channelled effectively.

house A symbolic division of your own birth chart into 12 areas corresponding in meaning approximately with the characteristics of the 12 zodiac signs.

house system A method of dividing the birth chart into houses. The Equal House system is one of the oldest and most straightforward systems to apply.

imum coeli Opposite from the midheaven and known technically as the point of lower culmination. Often abbreviated as the IC, from the Latin meaning "the bottom of the sky."

major aspect Conjunctions, sextiles, squares, trines and oppositions are major aspects, those in most frequent usage.

midheaven Known technically as the point of upper culmination, this is the highest point that the planets reach. Often abbreviated as the MC, from the Latin Medium Coeli, meaning "the middle of the sky."

midpoint A point halfway in zodiacal terms between two chart features.

minor aspect A whole range of aspects less frequently used, some of which are outlined in this book. The inconjunct is perhaps the most important minor aspect.

mutable Term used to describe the signs of Gemini, Virgo, Sagittarius and Pisces, known for their adaptable natures.

mutual reception Term used when each of two planets is found in the sign ruled by the other. This brings the planets into a good relationship, even if no precise aspect is formed.

negative signs The signs belonging to the earth and water elements are described collectively as negative, feminine or receptive.

north node Usually the Moon's north node, the point at which the orbit of the Moon around the Earth intersects with the orbit of the Earth around the Sun, when traveling northward from below the Earth's orbit.

orb of influence A spread of a few degrees either side of exactitude within which an aspect is still said to be in effect.

Part of Fortune Point derived from your unique combination of Sun, Moon and ascendant placings showing where and in what manner your greatest joy and happiness will be found.

planet To astronomers, a sizeable object orbiting the Sun. Astrologers in practice use this term to include the Sun and Moon as well.

polarity signs A pair of signs opposite each other in the zodiac.

positive signs The signs belonging to the elements of fire and air are often described as positive, masculine and active.

progression Method of advancing your birth chart year by year for long-term forecasting.

quadruplicity Cardinal, fixed or mutable. A method of categorizing the 12 signs into three groups of four, according to characteristics that they share.

quality Cardinal, fixed or mutable. An alternative term for quadruplicity.

retrograde The apparent reverse motion of a planet through the zodiac, caused by changes in our own perspective from an Earth that is also moving.

rising planet The closest planet to your ascendant, so long as it is within eight degrees.

rising sign An alternative term for your ascendant.

ruling planet The planet that rules your ascending sign.

secta Term used when dividing the signs into two groups, called positive and negative, masculine and feminine or active and receptive.

sidereal time The time by the stars used for calculating your ascendant and midheaven.

sign One of 12 zodiac constellations located in the part of the sky through which the planets move.

soft aspect Sextiles and trines are known as soft aspects and are inherently beneficial in their expression.

stellium Plural: stellia. A cluster of three or more planets in one house or sign.

synastry A technique used for assessing compatibility. The birth chart of one partner is superimposed onto the birth chart of the other so that the interaction between the two charts can be assessed.

table of houses Reference source, usually in book form, which lists the ascendant degree and midheaven for different times and locations.

transit A planetary movement, but often used to describe a predictive technique, based around the ongoing motion of the planets relative to your birth chart.

triplicity The division of the 12 signs into four groups of three, otherwise known as the elements.

INDEX

ACKNOWLEDGMENTS

Executive Editor Sandra Rigby
Managing Editor Clare Churly
Executive Art Editor Sally Bond
Designer James Lawrence
Illustrators Kuo Kang Chen, John Woodcock
Production Controller Simone Nauerth